The Prophetic Gifts & Office

A Biblical Perspective

by Steven Lambert, ThD

The Prophetic Gifs and Office — A Biblical Perspective
By Steven Lambert, ThD
ISBN 1-887915-03-6

Copyright © 1997, Real Truth Publications. All rights reserved under International Copyright Law. Contents and/or cover may not be reproduced in whole or in part in any form without the express written consent of the publisher who may be contacted at:

Real Truth Publications
P.O. Box 744
Jupiter, FL 33468-0744
(561) 624-8096
Email: slambert@slm.org
Website: www.slm.org

Unless otherwise indicated, the Bible text used in this publication is The *New American Standard Bible*, copyright © 1960, 1962, 1963, 1968, 1971, 1972, 1973, 1975, 1977, 1988; The Lockman Foundation. All rights reserved. Used by permission.

Printed in the United States of America.

A SPECIAL WORD TO THE READER

This course is not comprised of mere abstract theological *information* derived through *research*, but rather Spirit-inspired *illumination* about the prophetic realm derived from *revelation* of the Spirit and the Word of God as well as practical experience. The author is not merely a writer, researcher, or academe, but rather a prophet who has been functioning in the prophetic realm for more than twenty-five years, at the time of this writing, earnestly attempting to further expand his understanding of the prophetic and hone his own prophetic giftings. Notwithstanding, the conceptualization, historical orientation, and expression of the divinely-communicated revelation and understanding has been aided and augmented by the writings and teaching of other expositors on the main as well as collateral topics.

As you make your way through this study manual, please keep in mind it was written as a study guide, or syllabus, and is intended to be accompanied by expository teaching of the material. If, however, you are studying this manual on your own without an instructor, it is vital that you actually look up and study the cited Scripture references. The teaching by the author on audio cassettes may be obtained for $38.00 per set (includes applicable tax and shipping and handling). Simply send your request along with payment or credit card information (issuee name, address, phone number, card number and expiration date) to:

Real Truth Publications
P.O. Box 744
Jupiter, Florida 33468-0744
(561) 624-8096

ABOUT THE AUTHOR

DR. STEVEN LAMBERT is an ordained minister and holds several theological degrees. He has been in the ministry since 1977 as an apostolic prophet, teacher, conference and seminar speaker, pastor, and counselor. He is the author of an ever-increasing number of books, booklets, Bible courses, and study manuals. The two-fold emphasis of his ministry is the purification of the Church, in order that individual believers and the collective Church become "conformed into the Image of Christ" (Rom. 8:29), and restoration or restructure of the remnant Church that Jesus is building to conformity with the Divine Architectural Blueprint revealed in the God's Word. Dr. Lambert's prophetic ministry is a proven ministry. The countless prophetic words he has ministered over more than twenty-five years of prophetic ministry, besides being attested as accurate, have been a source of tremendous blessing, joy, edification, exhortation, and consolation unto thousands of recipients. As the Director of *Vision International Ministerial Association* and *Vision International University of Florida* he also works with other Fivefold ministers in developing their ministry gifts and ministries, and the equipping, training, and mentoring of ministers, counselors, and Christian workers within the local church.

Dr. Lambert may be contacted at:
   SLM, Inc
   P.O. Box 744
   Jupiter, FL 33468-0744
   (561) 624-8096

TABLE OF CONTENTS

FOREWARD i

SECTION I: INTRODUCTION TO THE PROPHETIC REALM

LESSON 1: Introduction To The Prophetic Realm (Part I) 1
LESSON 2: Introduction To The Prophetic Realm (Part II) 5

SECTION II: PROPHETS IN THE PLANS OF GOD

LESSON 3: The Place of Prophets In The Heart Of God 9
LESSON 4: The Participation Of Prophets In The Plans of God (Part I) 11
LESSON 5: The Participation Of Prophets In The Plans of God (Part II) 13
LESSON 6: The Participation Of Prophets In The Plans of God (Part III) 15
LESSON 7: The Participation Of Prophets In The Plans of God (Part IV) 17

SECTION III: THE ESTABLISHMENT OF THE PROPHET IN THE CHURCH

LESSON 8: The Shadow: The Ascension Of Elijah 19
LESSON 9: The Fulfillment: The Ascension Of Christ (Part I) 23
LESSON 10: The Fulfillment: The Ascension Of Christ (Part II) 27
LESSON 11: The Validity Of The Prophetic Office In The New Testament Church 31

SECTION IV: DETERIORATION AND RESTORATION IN THE CHURCH

LESSON 12: The Demise Of The Ministry Gifts 37
LESSON 13: The Restoration 43

SECTION V: THE COMING RESTORATION AND PURIFICATION

LESSON 14: Restoration And Reformation 51
LESSON 15: Purification And Glorification 57
LESSON 16: The Elijah Company Of Prophets in the Coming Restoration and Purification 61
LESSON 17: Restoration, Reformation, Revolution, and Resisters 67

SECTION VI: THE PROPHETIC GIFTS AND OFFICE

LESSON 18: Gifts Vs. Office 75
LESSON 19: The Ministry Of The Prophet 81
LESSON 20: The Gift Of Prophecy 87
LESSON 21: The Manifestation Gift Of Tongues 97

SECTION VII: ABOUT PERSONAL PROPHECY

LESSON 22: All About Personal Prophecy 101

FOREWARD

FOREWARD

"...be established in the **PRESENT TRUTH.**" (1 Pet. 1:12)

"**...as for knowledge,** it will pass away [that is, it will lose its value and **be superseded by truth].** For our knowledge is fragmentary (incomplete and imperfect), and our prophecy (our teaching) is fragmentary (incomplete and imperfect). **But when the complete and perfect [total] comes, the incomplete and imperfect will vanish away — become antiquated, void and superseded....**For now we are looking in a mirror that gives only a dim (blurred) reflection [of reality as in a riddle or enigma], but then [when perfection comes] we shall see in reality and face to face! **Now I know in part (imperfectly); but then I shall know and understand fully and clearly,** even in the same manner as I have been fully and clearly known and understood [by God]." (1 Cor. 13:8-12, Amplified Bible)

The entrance of Gods Word gives light, or illumination of the Truth (Ps. 119:130). By and by, through the centuries, God has been progressively dispelling spiritual darkness in the Church by gradually revealing more and more Truth and gradually granting greater illumination of the Truth. As a result, the Church's understanding of what Truth is, is becoming more and more complete and perfected as we approach the end of the Church Age. This is the import of the Divine exhortation that we "be established in **PRESENT Truth**" (2 Pet. 1:12, KJV). Certainly the Truth as it exists in the Mind of God is absolute and absolutely perfect, and therefore cannot be improved or upgraded. Rather, it is the Church's **understanding** of the Truth that is constantly being improved and upgraded. Ever since its birth, the Lord has been teaching and maturing the Church, renewing our collective mind to make it to be congruous with the "mind of Christ." That process continues in these last days as the Holy Spirit dispels the darkness which has been blinding our eyes and elucidates Truth which in a semantic sense is "new" but which in reality is not, since it has really been there all along.

As the above Corinthian passage indicates, especially in the Amplified Bible's paraphrase, partial and incomplete knowledge is continuously being superseded by more perfect, or more complete, knowledge as the Lord bestows greater illumination of the Truth. As a part of that more perfect knowledge, the Lord is now revealing fresh illumination of the Truth regarding the matter of the **PROPHETIC** gifts and office.

The Charismatic Movement brought forth a restoration of and renewed awareness in the "Charismata" or Manifestation Gifts of the Spirit. However, as it happened, the main focus of that renewed awareness was the revelation and power gifts. Though there was a smattering of teaching on and sporadic employment of the prophetic giftings in some circles during that move, the prophetic realm was generally less explored and expounded upon, plus, the prophetic arm of the Church remained largely undeveloped and untapped, and was kept at an arm's distance. For the most part, it was as though the matter of the prophetic realm remained a "sealed" chapter in the book of Divine revelation knowledge.

But, how wondrous are the ways of God! After all the centuries transpiring since the Church fell into the Dark Ages, the winds of restoration and reformation are once again blowing throughout Christendom. God is bringing fresh revelation and illumination concerning this previously neglected and greatly misunderstood area of Truth, and has initiated a restorational period in which the prophetic realm is being reestablished within the Church. These Restorational Winds are stirring up new and added interest in the prophetic office and gifts. Ordinary believers and church leaders alike are being motivated by a God-caused hunger to become more knowledgeable of and activated in this powerful realm of the Spirit—the prophetic realm. Prophets and prophetic teachers are now disseminating through various media greatly needed teaching on this intriguing and unique area of ministry.

Until very recently, if someone would have dared to call himself a "prophet," in most circles he would have been ridiculed, censured, castigated, ostracized, and even branded a heretic. Now, that is beginning to change. Though, as in the case of every other restorational move of God, there will undoubtedly be "stiff-necked resisters of the Holy Spirit" (Ac. 7:51) who will resist the purposes of God, and persecute the emerging leaders of this God-ordained emphasis and attempt to subvert their efforts, even if successful, they will be powerless to withstand or suppress the great tidal wave of restoration and reformation that is coming!

A new day has dawned for the Church of the Lord Jesus Christ! Jesus is personally coming to visit His Church and those groups and ministries that claim to be part of His Church. Just as He stood outside the door of the First Century churches, knocking, seeking to be granted entrance (Rev. 3:20), so also Jesus is standing outside the door of the lukewarm and self-absorbed churches of this Laodicean Age, knocking, and waiting to see if they will open the door and bid Him entrance. However, many will not recognize Him as He comes during this era of restoration in a different form (Mk. 16:12) as the **Preeminent Prophet**, and will thus refuse to open the door and allow Him entrance. As they did in the days of His fleshly ministry, so also today, many religious people will call the Head of the House—Beezelbul!

However, there are an ever-increasing number of church leaders who are earnestly seeking God for answers as they realize their churches and ministries are facing serious problems that can no longer be remedied by the Madison Avenue techniques and Wall Street formulas promulgated by the so-called "church growth" experts of recent note—problems which in many cases threaten the very viability of their churches and ministries. Many are also coming to recognize in all honesty that God never was sponsoring many of the church programs and projects they once claimed He had inspired. Indeed, this is a day of great introspection and prayerful reexamination for all true lampstand (Rev. 1:20) church organizations and ministries.

Because of a host of recent developments and dilemmas ministries are now facing, in frustration and desperation, some church leaders are beginning to truly seek the face of God and are becoming more and more willing to tap into the powerful source of God-inspired direction and guidance the prophetic gifts and office have always been. In time, earnest and sincere leaders are going to begin to call for God's prophets in order to hear the pure and unadulterated Word of the Wonderful Counselor. As that happens, in the passage of time, God's true, tried, and trained prophets will come to be less and less **dis**regarded and **dis**dained, and will be highly re**gard**ed as the **or**dained messengers of God they have always been. Rather than being regarded as the **foe** and rejected, God's surrogate spokesmen will eventually be received as the greatly needed **friend** of the Church and of God Himself they have always been in truth.

The Word of God makes it clear that Fivefold ministry functioning and flowing together in concerted effort to complete the maturing of the Church unto Christ-like stature is a mandate from God (Eph. 4:11-13). **Three**-Fold ministry consisting only of Evangelists, Pastors, and Teachers is incapable of accomplishing the task of fully maturing the Church and bringing it into conformity with the Image of Christ (Rom. 8:29). Present-Truth as it pertains to the Fivefold ministry, which includes the effectual functioning of Apostles and Prophets today, can no longer be ignored by ministers and ministries desiring to be established upon the Solid Rock of Present-Truth. Churches and ministries that attempt to defy God and continue to ignore the reality of Fivefold ministry will fail, fall, and become dysfunctional.

Jesus is building **HIS** Church in accordance with **HIS** architectural blueprint, the specifications of which require that the Building be established upon the foundation of the ministry offices of the Apostle and Prophet (Eph 2:20). And, it is against **this** Church—the one Jesus Himself is building, the one that has as its foundation the ministries of the Apostles and Prophets—that the gates (powers) of hell shall not be able to prevail. Conversely, Churches not so built will be vanquished by the forces of hell.

Make no mistake about it! God's winnowing fork is in His hand to thoroughly purge His threshing floor of all the chaff and all the tares. He is now in the process of separating the true docile Sheep of His Flock from the derelict goats. He is raising up a Company of End-Time Apostles and Prophets who will usher in the last great Tidal Wave of restoration and reformation within the Church, which, when it has accomplished its purposes, will culminate in the return of Jesus Christ to claim the purified Church as His Eternal Bride and the Marriage Supper of the Lamb!

It is on the backdrop of all this that this study manual was written. Its content is predicated first and foremost on Scripture, but also on a considerable number of years of firsthand practical experience in prophetic ministry. The purpose of the manual simply is to provide systematic teaching regarding the specter of the prophetic that is informative and helpful to anyone desirous of becoming more knowledgeable regarding this unique realm of the Spirit. A secondary hope is that the information presented in this study manual will make some contribution toward allaying the unwarranted fear regarding the prophetic common to so many, due primarily to extensive lack of knowledge.

The sole motivation for composing this study manual was a profound and abiding love and appreciation for the prophetic endowments. My greatest desire is that all who sojourn these pages be edified, encouraged, better educated, and better equipped to effectively minister on behalf of Jesus via the prophetic gifts and office unto the billions of hurting and needy people dotting this planet; for "one who prophesies **EDIFIES**..." (1 Cor. 14:3).

My personal sentiments regarding this wonderful specter of the Spirit are wonderfully represented in the words of two great prophetic men of the Bible—the Apostle Paul, who exhorted **all** believers: **"COVET to prophesy"** (1 Cor. 14:1), and the great Prophet Moses, who declared, "I would to God that **ALL** the Lord's people were **PROPHETIC PEOPLE**" (Num. 11:29, paraphrased).

Steven Lambert, ThD
Apostolic Prophet

SECTION I:
INTRODUCTION TO THE PROPHETIC REALM

LESSON 1:
INTRODUCTION TO THE PROPHETIC REALM
(PART I)

GOD'S BASIC DESIRE FOR INTERCOMMUNICATION AND FELLOWSHIP

God's very purpose for creating mankind was personal, intimate fellowship and intercommunication. In this last day as well, God has not become mute, but is adamant about maintaining communication and fellowship with His mankind creation.

He has always wanted to communicate with us. He is looking for those who will listen for His communication. He is speaking much more than most people are listening.

The problem is not that God is not speaking, but that most people are not listening and have not learned how to hear the Lord's divine communication.

God employs many means of communication, and certainly does not limit Himself to only one. He will use whatever means necessary to communicate His message, will, and purposes unto people. In the Bible He spoke through people, angels, a burning bush, through circumstances, through supernatural acts, and He even spoke through a dumb donkey once.

DIRECT COMMUNICATION in the Garden of Eden—Gen. 3:8-19

God walked and talked (fellowshipped) with Adam and Eve in the Garden of Eden prior to their disobedience and fall. Thus, Man in his original spiritual estate enjoyed direct, personal communication with God.

MAN DISOBEYED GOD'S WORD AND FELL, and thereby **LOST** their **FELLOWSHIP WITH GOD** and the **DIVINE NATURE OF GOD (2 Pet. 1:4)** and received the **CARNAL NATURE OF SATAN (Eph. 2:1-3).**

Is. 6:1-10 The consequence of the disobedience and fall of man was that human **spiritual hearing and sight** (insight) **was greatly DULLED** and man was rendered **spiritually INSENSITIVE** to the voice of God.

SECOND ADAM (JESUS) RESTORED OUR SPIRITUAL COMMUNICATION WITH GOD

1 Jn. 3:8 Jesus came as the **Second Adam** to REVERSE THE CURSE! He came to redeem man from the effects of sin which the first Adam brought upon all of mankind through his disobedience.

Mat. 27:50,51; 2 Cor. 3:14-16 By His substitutionary death, Jesus rent the veil that was placed over our spiritual eyes through Adam's sin, restoring our ability to see into the spiritual realm.

A Biblical Perspective of the Prophetic Gifts and Office

1 Cor. 13:9-12 However, because the sin nature has not been totally eradicated from us, we still look through a dark glass dimly; know only in part; and prophesy only in part. Our knowledge is not yet complete, but is only partial. We only know that which God chooses to reveal to us by the Spirit. The attainment of true spiritual knowledge and understanding is progressive. Knowing how to hear from God is a process that no believer is perfected in yet, and never will be until we receive our full redemption.

Heb. 5:14 **Understanding how to and becoming adept at RECOGNIZING** the voice of the Lord is an on-going learning process, which is only perfected through years of practice in training one's spiritual senses. Fortunately, while we are in that process, **the Lord has not limited Himself to inward intercommunication exclusively.**

JESUS—the exact Expression of God.

Heb. 1:1,2 In the fulness of time, God spoke to us in the person of Jesus Christ. Yet, as we shall see later, this text is in no wise indicating that the need for prophetic people and prophecy was eliminated by the coming of Jesus. On the contrary, Jesus Himself established prophets and the prophetic in the Church.

1 Tim. 3:16 Jesus was God Himself manifest in the flesh.

Jn. 14:5,11; Col. 2:9 Jesus was the first and **Preeminent Prophet,** but was and is **much more than a Prophet**. He was the **exact and complete expression** of God Himself in bodily form.

Jn. 1:1-14; 1 Jn. 1:1-3; Heb. 1:3 Jesus was the embodiment of the very word, will, and wisdom of God manifested on Earth.

Rom. 8:29; 1 Pet. 2:9,10 Jesus was the first-born of a new race of God-created beings, the Children of God, who are in the process of being conformed to His image and likeness.

THE HOLY SPIRIT—divine intercommunications.

Jn. 14:18,19 After Jesus' bodily ascension to Heaven, the fullness of God in bodily form was no longer visible to the **world**.

Jn. 16:7 However, Jesus did not leave us **fatherless,** i.e., without fatherly guidance and instruction—**He sent the Holy Spirit** to be our "Paracletos" (Helper).

Jn. 16:13-15; Jn. 14:25,26 The Holy Spirit is the **Spirit of Truth**. His role is to guide us into all spiritual Truth.

1 Cor. 2:6-10 The very purpose of **Jesus' vicarious death** was **to restore our fellowship with God and our spiritual hearing and insight**. As a result, we now have the "mind of Christ" through the Spirit to know the mysteries and the very depths of God.

THE LOGOS (The Bible)—God in Written Form.

2 Pet. 1:20,21; Eph. 3:5 The Holy Spirit inspired the writing of the Bible through Apostles and Prophets.

A Biblical Perspective of the Prophetic Gifts and Office

2 Tim. 3:15-17 The Bible is the complete revelation of the **general will** of God. The Bible is a closed canon, consisting of sixty-six books. In no way is it being said or inferred that prophetic ministry adds to or subtracts from the Bible; Scripture strictly prohibits that. Rather, prophets are often used by God as His special messengers to convey inspired **illumination, instruction, and application** concerning the Word of God **(Eph. 3:1-10)**. Most people are not doing much of what is written in the sixty-six books that comprise the Bible, so we certainly don't need any more to be added to it.

THE PROPHETIC VOICE OF THE HOLY SPIRIT — God Speaking Through Human Channels.

Rom. 8:14 "For all who are being led by the Spirit of God, these are **SONS** of God."

This passage indicates that Born Again believers are to be led (guided) by the Holy Spirit. As we have seen, the Holy Spirit can lead us and communicate with us through the written Word of God (Logos) as well as by direct inward communication. But, He has not limited Himself to those two forms of communication. He also speaks to us through other human vessels.

The Greek word translated "sons" in this passage is the word **"huios"** which refers to "**mature** sons" as distinguished from mere children of God. While every Born Again believer is a "child of God," it takes some development over time to become a "mature son" of God. Those who have reached some level of maturity, begin to hear from God on their own; but "babes" do not, they aren't mature enough to do so.

Yet, even when we have begun to mature, and even in the case of some of the most mature believers, there are times when, for various reasons, we simply cannot hear for ourselves the pure Word of the Lord unto us. It is at those times that we need to allow the Lord, if He chooses to do so, to communicate to us by the "prophetic voice of the Holy Spirit" through other believers of His choosing. This is one of many ways in which the Lord keeps us ever mindful of our need for one another and the realization that no believer will ever become self-sufficient or self-dependent in his relationship with God.

1 Cor. 3:16 We all need the other members of the Body of Christ! It is the collective "WE" of the Body of Christ who have "the mind of Christ," not any one individual believer independent of the rest of the Body! Individual completeness independent of other believers is neither a reality, nor even a valid goal.

While it is certainly true that God desires to walk and talk with us directly in personal and intimate fellowship through the Bible and through inward communication from the Holy Spirit, **that does not negate human channels of communication.**

The coming of the Messiah, His sending of the Holy Spirit upon His departure, the birth of the Church, and even the writing of the Bible did not eliminate the need for or the validity of the prophetic voice of the Lord through human channels. In fact, the need for the prophetic voice of the Lord was irrevocably established as a valid and needful operation within the Church for the duration of the Church Age by Jesus Himself as the Head of the Church, by the Holy Spirit speaking through the New Testament writers, and by Holy Scripture itself.

Acts 2:17 Peter interpreted the "**THOSE DAYS**" of which the Prophet Joel prophesied as being the **CHURCH AGE** in his prophesy: "I will pour out of My Spirit **IN THOSE DAYS**, and your sons and your daughters shall **PROPHESY**."

1 Cor. 14:39 **AFTER** the Holy Spirit had come and **AFTER** the Birth of the Church on the Day of Pentecost, the Apostle Paul by inspiration of the Holy Spirit Himself commanded all believers throughout the Church Age to **"covet to prophesy,"** thereby establishing the vocalization of the "Rhema Word of God" through human channels as a **valid New Testament medium** of communication from God for the duration of the Church Age.

1 Cor. 12:28, Eph. 4:7-11 Additionally, it was **AFTER** Jesus had come as the Messiah and completed His priestly mission when He was ascending on high to take His Seat at the right hand of God that He relegated the Fivefold ministry gifts, including **prophets**, as permanent functions within the Church. Thus, the **motivation** gift of prophecy **(Rom 12:6)**, the **manifestation** gift of prophecy [which includes tongues and interpretation of tongues] **(1 Cor. 12:10)**, and the **ministry** gift of prophet were all established as valid New Testament giftings.

So God has set within the Body three major media of the voice of the Spirit:

the gift of prophecy as the voice of the Holy Spirit in the midst of the congregation;

spirit of prophecy as the testimony of Jesus Himself;

the ministry of the prophet as a special surrogate voice, speaking divine communication on behalf of God.

LESSON 2
INTRODUCTION TO THE PROPHETIC REALM
(PART II)

NOTE: This lesson contains only a simplistic overview of these media of the voice of the Holy Spirit. Each will be discussed in greater depth in later lessons.

THE GIFT OF PROPHECY — The Voice of the Holy Spirit in the midst of the congregation (1 Cor. 12:10).

1 Cor. 12:7,11 The **Gift of Prophecy** is a vocal manifestation of the Holy Spirit of the thoughts, will, and counsel of God, given for the common good of the hearers through any willing
Spirit-filled believer He wills to use.

1 Cor. 14:3 The simple **gift of prophecy** operating through a **saint** must **ALWAYS** be unto and limited to **edification, exhortation,** and **comfort.** A "lay-saint" (i.e., a saint not in a Fivefold ministry office) **must never attempt to bring guidance, direction, correction, admonition, or instruction** through the exercise of a so-called "prophecy." Those duties should be left to those appointed to the office of **Prophet.**

1 Cor. 14:40 In order to be a valid operation of the gift of prophecy it must always be **"done decently and in order."**

1 Cor. 14:1 Every believer should **"covet to prophesy."**

1 Tim. 4:14 Believers should not neglect the spiritual gifts activated within them, but should **"stir up"** those gifts and not allow them to fall into disuse **(2 Tim. 1:6).**

THE SPIRIT OF PROPHECY — the testimony of Jesus Himself.

Rev. 19:10 The **spirit of prophecy** is the **testimony of Jesus.**

Num. 11:16-29, 1 Sam. 10:1-11 The Lord, at His discretion, may relegate the "Spirit of Prophecy" that is upon a PROPHET (the OFFICE) unto a cadre of delegated leaders functioning under the auspices and authority of that prophet. Moreover, it is common for the "Spirit of Prophecy" to be abnormally activated in gatherings in which a prophet is present or is presiding.

Heb. 2:12 The **song of the Lord** — Jesus singing in the midst of the congregation through a saint.

1 Chron. 25:1-3; 2 Chron. 5:11-14 **Prophetic worship**.

2 Kgs. 3:15 **Prophetic anointing** through anointed music.

SECTION I: INTRODUCTION TO THE PROPHETIC REALM

THE MINISTRY (OFFICE) OF THE PROPHET—a special surrogate voice, speaking Divine communication on behalf of God.

God has always desired that the revelation of His will be expressed. Thus, He has established **the MINISTRY (OFFICE) of the prophet** as a channel for the **revelation and illumination** of His Word, Will, and Ways; **specific instruction concerning His personal will** for individuals; and, **confirmation and witness** of God's leading.

Simply defined, the Prophet is God's spokesman. **The** term **"Prophet"** connotes: "to speak on behalf of" — from "pro" = on behalf of / "phet" = to speak.

Ex. 20:18-21; Deut. 18:15-19 Patriarchs and Prophets—God raised up **after the fall** as His personal spokesmen to mankind in order to communicate more clearly and effectively with man.

Prophetic ministry and **the voice of the prophet** were established by God as His primary medium of communication with fallen man on planet earth, prior to the coming of Jesus.

Some people erroneously think there is not much in the Bible about prophets and the prophetic realm, demonstrating their ignorance of Scripture. The following is an accounting of **references in Scripture to prophets and the prophetic:**

> **Total references** to prophets and the prophetic **638**
>   Old Testament 443
>   New Testament 195
>
> Total **prophets** of God referenced in Scripture (excluding "false prophets") **77**
>   Old Testament 46
>   New Testament 31
>   (e.g., Jesus, Adam, Abraham, Isaac, Jacob, Joseph, Moses, Aaron, Joshua, Samuel, David, Solomon, Elijah, Elisha, all the O.T. major/minor prophets, 24 N.T. Apostles, et al.)
>
> Total **prophetesses** named in Scripture **11**
>   (e.g., Miriam, Huldah, Noadiah, Isaiah's Wife, Elizabeth, Anna, 4 Daughters of Philip)

2 Pet. 1:20,21 ALL of Scripture was written by **PROPHETS**.

Adam, the very first man, was a Prophet—he spoke on behalf of God to his wife.

Abraham is the first to be called **"a prophet"** in Scripture **(Gen. 20:7)**, and it was God Himself that called Him that; thus God Himself invented the term.

ALL of the **PATRIARCHS** were prophets. They **prophesied in part (1 Cor. 13:9)**, often speaking words they themselves did not fully comprehend.

Moses, the type and foreshadow of the Messiah, was a prophet, and said the **Messiah** would be a Prophet **(Dt. 18:15)**.

A Biblical Perspective of the Prophetic Gifts and Office

The tool of the Prophet—Personal Prophecy.

2 Cor. 13:1 God says that every word must be **confirmed** by the mouth of **two or three witnesses. The prophetic voice often fulfills this critical role**, especially when it comes through prophets.

Personal prophecy, however, must never become or be used as a **substitute** for the **personal responsibility and privilege** of hearing the voice of God for one's self. Prophets must never be viewed as "mediums" or "mediators" between God and people. Believers are enjoined to fast, pray, and read their Bible in order to seek and to hear from God for themselves. There can be no substitutes for those elements of intimate fellowship and communion with God, not even valid giftings, for **He is a jealous God**.

Nevertheless, for various reasons, many people still do not hear God for themselves. So God often uses **THE VOICE OF THE PROPHET (office)** and **PERSONAL PROPHECY (gift)** to communicate His Rhema Word to **individuals**, **groups**, and even whole **nations**.

Prophecy is intended to be used for construction, not destruction! It certainly is nothing to play with! It has the potential, when used properly, to be a tremendous source of blessing. However, when used improperly by the inexperienced, immature, or ill-motivated, it can produce disastrous and extremely injurious results.

One of the greatest problems that will arise during this movement in which the prophetic gifts are being reactivated and re-emphasized will be the devaluation of prophecy as a result of misuse and abuse of prophetic giftings by selfishly-motivated novices who will attempt to use them as a means by which to draw attention to themselves, to impress others with their "spirituality," and to satisfy their need to feel important.

While many are nearly obsessed with fear of being deceived by "false prophets," the greatest damage that will be done in this realm will not come from truly called and anointed *ministers* operating in the prophetic giftings, but by untrained, self-appointed *lay-believers* who have "zeal without knowledge" and who "think more highly of themselves than they ought" (**Rom. 12:3**) in terms of their own callings and giftings.

By no means, however, is that to say that there will not be a contingency of false prophets who will arise and misuse and abuse the prophetic gifts and office for selfish-gain of various forms. There will certainly be many of those plaguing the church as well, but still the greatest numbers of wrongly-motivated "prophesiers" causing consternation and confusion among believers will come not from the *pulpits* but from the *pews*; that is, not from the ranks of *leadership* but the *laity*. Regardless of the rank of function of the perpetrator, the primary indicator that someone is a "false prophet," Jesus said, was that they were "ravenous wolves," or in other words, their inward motivations were bent toward selfish-gain, and they use the prophetic for self-aggrandizing purposes rather than to glorify Christ as does valid prophetic function.

(*The topics of Prophets and Personal Prophecy will be discussed in depth in a future lesson.*)

A Biblical Perspective of the Prophetic Gifts and Office

SECTION II:

THE PLACE OF PROPHETS IN THE PLANS OF GOD

LESSON 3
THE PLACE OF PROPHETS IN THE HEART OF GOD

PROPHETS OCCUPY A SPECIAL PLACE IN THE HEART OF GOD

Though God is no respecter of persons, He seems to have a **special affection** for His true prophets and expresses **special concern** for their plight. Evidence of this is found in some of God's unique declarations and admonitions regarding His prophets, such as—

to **touch** (afflict, persecute, oppose) them not and do them **no harm (Ps. 105:15);**

to **touch** one or even a member of his family in an inappropriate or disrespectful way is to touch the apple of His eye, and is sin against God **(Gen. 20:7);**

that curses will come upon those who **curse** or **castigate** or **scorn** them **(2 Kgs. 2:23,24);**

that whoever **receives** a prophet in the name of a prophet is **receiving JESUS** Himself and will receive a **prophet's reward (Mat. 10:40,41).**

God is so attune to the plight of, and personally angered by, the mistreatment His **prophets** usually suffer, that He has promised to **avenge the blood** of the prophets **(Rev. 16:6; 18:20-24).**

GOD DOES NOT WANT THE PROPHETIC MINISTRY THWARTED

The role and responsibility of bonafide, God-appointed prophets is literally to speak on behalf of God. Hence, He warns against anyone thwarting their ministry. God's admonition against hindering or rejecting prophetic ministry and the ministry of His prophets is poignant and clear. He says:

to **reject** bonafide, God appointed prophets is to reject **God (1 Sam. 8:7);**

to **prohibit** prophets from speaking is to prohibit **God** from speaking **(Deut. 18:15);**

to **permit** the prophets to speak what God is inspiring them to speak **(1 Cor. 14:29);**

to **despise not** prophesying **(1 Thes. 5:20);**

the **spirit of prophecy** is the **testimony of JESUS Himself**, not of any man **(Rev. 19:10).**

GOD PLEDGES UNIQUE PROMISES OF PERFORMANCE THROUGH THE PROPHETIC MINISTRY

There are numerous statements in the Bible which indicate the uniqueness of the prophetic ministry; for example:

A Biblical Perspective of the Prophetic Gifts and Office

2 Chr. 20:20 God promises **success and prosperity** to those who believe the Word of God uttered through the mouth of **prophets.**

Is. 44:26 God pledges to **confirm the Word** of His servants, the **prophets**, and to **perform the purpose** of His messengers.

Amos 3:7 God says He **reveals His secret plans and counsel** unto His servants, the **prophets**.

Important Note: This volume is a study of the prophetic gifts and office. Concerning scriptural declarations regarding prophets and the prophetic gifts addressed here and throughout this manual, it is important to keep the following factors in mind with respect to practical application of the various points discussed herein.

First, every bonafide, born again believer is a member of the Body of Christ, having been baptized by the Spirit into the Body (1 Cor. 12:13). God now dwells in each and every one of us believers. We literally are now the Temple or tabernacle of God. The veil separating us from intimate and personal fellowship and communion with God was rent from top to bottom two thousand years ago at the very moment when the Lamb of God cried out through the darkness, "It is finished!" With the veil removed, each of us has abundant access into the Holy of Holies ourselves, and the Spirit of the Lord, who formerly spoke only through the Old Testament Prophets, now indwells every believer. Thus, quite different than the Old Testament scenario, all believers, whether Fivefold minister or layman, are now "on the same level as brothers" (Mat. 23:8; L.B.), especially in terms of our access and fellowship (communion and communication) with God. Hence, in this sense, the only diversity that exists among believers is that of *function* and not in regard to *fellowship* with God.

Second, now, in the New Testament dispensation, we are under the law of love and grace rather than the Mosaic Law of condemnation that was in effect during the Old Testament era. This accounts for a number of differences regarding the prophetic now in contrast to the Old Testament period. One salient difference, one that critics of the prophetic gifts and office being operable today, commonly known as "cessasionists," are want to reference in their criticisms, is that we no longer stone those who purport to speak prophetically and whose prophecy does not turn out to have been one-hundred percent accurate. In fact doing so would obviously be punishable under civil law as murder, not to mention the fact that such contempt for a fellow believer under God's Law of Love IS murder (1 Jn. 3:15)

Third, when Jesus ascended on high (Eph 4:7) He expanded the one ministry office that existed in the Old Testament era — the prophetic office — and distributed out of it three additional ministry giftings (evangelists, pastors, teachers) to "speak on behalf of God," each in the uniqeness indigenous to that office and gifting. While the word "prophet," as pointed out in this manual, literally means "to speak on behalf of God," *all* ministers speak on behalf of God in a different way. Jesus established the apostolic office during the Intertestamental era, when He chose and appointed the Twelve Apostles of the Lamb. Each of the fivefold ministry offices, the seven motivation giftings, as well as the twelve manifestation gifts is just as important and vital as the others. In no way, is the intent of this volume to vaunt the prophetic gifts and office above any of the others. Once again, the focus of this manual is the prophetic realm.

A Biblical Perspective of the Prophetic Gifts and Office

LESSON 4
THE PARTICIPATION OF PROPHETS IN THE PLANS OF GOD THROUGHOUT THE AGES
(Part I)

PROPHETS PARTICIPATE IN ALL OF GOD'S PLANS AND PERFORMANCES.

Prophets have always been God's special messengers active in every Age to perform special tasks and assignments!

Prophets and the prophetic ministry are and will continue to be active in every age and dispensation of God's dealings with man, from the Garden of Eden and all the way through the ages to the very end of the Church Age and the final judgment—

Adam prophesied to his wife in the Garden of Eden before the fall of man **(Gen. 3:2,3)**;

Prophets and apostles are specifically addressed at the fall of Babylon, which was guilty of shedding the blood of the **prophets (Rev. 18:20,24).**

IN THE BEGINNING AGE (GENESIS)

Lk. 1:70 "He spake by the mouth of His holy **PROPHETS which have been SINCE THE WORLD BEGAN.**" Prophets have existed and been active in every age since the world began.

Gen. 3:2,3 ADAM, the first man, **prophesied to his wife** in the beginning of creation. **Adam was the first human prophet.**

DURING THE OLD COVENANT AGE

Gen. 20:7 ABRAHAM, the **first Patriarch** of the faith, and **ALL** of the **Patriarchs** were **prophets. Abraham** is the **first** to be called **"a prophet"** in Scripture, and it was God Himself that called Him that—thus, **God Himself invented the term.**

Deut. 18:15 MOSES, the type of the Messiah-Deliverer, was a **prophet,** and said the **Messiah** would be a **prophet.**

Under the Old Covenant, the **Prophet** was **God's primary means of communication** with His chosen people. Most all of His communication, both to the people and to their governing authorities, came primarily through His **prophets.** God Himself said He revealed His secret plans and counsel unto His servants, the **prophets (Amos 3:7),** who in turn related that counsel which the Lord wanted to be conveyed unto the people.

The Prophet's anointing upon the patriarchs of the faith enabled Adam, Enoch, Noah, Abraham, Isaac, Jacob, Moses, David, Solomon, and other great men of God, to perform many special tasks and assignments; such as to—

A Biblical Perspective of the Prophetic Gifts and Office

predict future happenings;

receive explicit instruction from God for new things He wanted to do and accomplish; such as in the case of the building of such things as Noah's ark, the ark of the covenant and the tabernacle of God for God's dwelling, the rebuilding of the walls of Jerusalem, et al;

receive supernatural insight from God concerning His divine plans, purposes, principles, ordinances (Moses and the Law), methods, means;

decree the prophetic future of their descendants;

receive revelations from God concerning the means and methods for deliverance of His people from bondage;

receive divine knowledge from God regarding vital national matters, such as those chosen and anointed by God for national leadership (the kings divinely appointed by God for kingship were anointed by a **prophet** for their installation into their office), impending famines, draughts, economic stresses, and eminent destructions, and even supernaturally revealed vital military intelligence (God pledged to reveal His secret plans and counsel unto His servants the **prophets [Amos 3:7]**).

record for all of posterity, the inspired account of **"HIS-STORY"** — the Bible. All of the Old Testament books were written by **prophets.** All of the New Testament books were written by Apostles (who were also **prophets**) or through their "amanuensis" (secretary). This matter of the writing of the Bible is an achievement which is, for the most part, greatly underestimated.

Prophets predicted and **prepared the way** for the coming of the Messiah. It was a **prophet** (so identified by Jesus Himself), John the Baptist, the natural cousin of the Messiah, who prepared the way for the coming of the Messiah, at the consummation of the Old Covenant Age and advent of the New.

Throughout all the ages, **prophets** have been God's voice to bring **repentance, reformation,** and **restoration** during divinely appointed "times of refreshing" and "times of restoration" **(Acts 3:18-21).**

Prophets will be **instruments** of God **to execute His judgments** at the consummation of the Church Age **(Rev. 11:3-13)**. (*More on this in Lesson 7.*)

A Biblical Perspective of the Prophetic Gifts and Office

LESSON 5
THE PARTICIPATION OF PROPHETS
IN THE PLANS OF GOD THROUGHOUT THE AGES
(Part II)

PROPHETS PARTICIPATE IN ALL OF GOD'S PLANS AND PERFORMANCES.

ALL THROUGHOUT THE CHURCH AGE

Heb. 1:1-3 In the fullness of time, God spoke to us in the person of Jesus Christ. Though Jesus was **much more than a Prophet**, He is indeed the **Preeminent Prophet**, through whom God now speaks, and Jesus has relegated His prophetic ministry unto underling prophets who speak in His stead.

Heb. 13:8 Jesus Christ (including the Body of Christ) is **the same** yesterday, today, and forever. Thus, because we are still in the Church Age, Apostles and Prophets are still for today.

Eph. 4:7-11 At the very genesis of the Church Age, the glorified Head of the Church, as He ascended to sit down at the right hand of the Father on His throne, delegated His ministry gift and anointing of **PROPHET** to particular members of the Church. Thus, **THE CHURCH AGE BEGAN WITH THE PROPHET ESTABLISHED IN THE CHURCH.** (More on this issue in Section III.)

Eph. 4:11-13 The ministry office of **Prophet has not been** abolished or abrogated, any more than any of the other Fivefold ministry offices have been. If the ministry office of the prophet is no longer valid, neither are any of the other ministry offices, because they all appear in the same verse. Hence, **Prophets** are to continue to be vitally **active and functioning,** along with the other ministry gifts, **ALL THROUGHOUT THE CHURCH AGE.**

1 Cor. 12:28 Prophets were set into the Church by God Himself and are an integral part of all God is doing on Earth. The term **"set"** in this passage testifies of the **permanence** of these local church presbytery offices. God has **never rescinded** the appointment of the Apostles and Prophets in the Church, according to the Bible; no where does it say He has.

THE PROPHET IS PART OF THE FOUNDATION OF THE CHURCH:

1 Cor. 3:11 Jesus Himself is the **FOUNDATION** of the Church.

Acts 3:22 Moses foretold that Jesus, the **MESSIAH**, would be a **PROPHET**.

Jn. 4:19 The woman at the well perceived rightly and confirmed the fact that Jesus, the Messiah, was a **PROPHET.** (This supposedly "unspiritual" Samaritan woman had more spiritual sense than many purported "spiritual" people today, for she knew a prophet when she encountered one.)

Col. 1:18 The **FIRST-BORN** from the dead, i.e., the first member of the Church, Jesus, was a **PROPHET**.

Rom. 8:29 The **FIRST-BORN** of the Church was a **PROPHET**. **Jesus Himself was the begin-ning of the Church Age.**

Eph. 5:23 The **HEAD** of the church is a **PROPHET**.

Eph. 2:20 Apostles and **prophets** are **the foundational ministries** of the Church in that they lay the foundation of Christ Himself in the collective Church as well as individual churches. In the same way that the apostles and prophets of the early Church gave **divine direction** to the early Church in its formative years, so the ministry of end-time apostles and prophets is to give divine direction from Jesus for the building of His Church through revelation and illumination of "the testimony of Jesus" (prophecy) unto the Church.

LESSON 6
THE PARTICIPATION OF PROPHETS
IN THE PLANS OF GOD THROUGHOUT THE AGES
(Part III)

PROPHETS PARTICIPATE IN ALL OF GOD'S PLANS AND PERFORMANCES.

ALL THROUGHOUT THE CHURCH AGE (Continued)

Acts 3:18-21 All throughout the Church Age, **Prophets** have been God's voice to bring **repentance, reformation,** and **restoration** during divinely appointed **"times of refreshing"** and **"times of restoration."**

There have been a number of men raised up by God since the last hundred years or so of the Dark Ages who have been used by God to bring repentance, reformation, restoration, and in some cases revolution. The nature of many of these men's ministries and labor indicate they were really **prophets**, though few were recognized as such. Some of the Dutch Reform Movement and the Protestant Movement (e.g., Wycliffe, Huss, Luther, et al.), the Holiness Movement, and so on right on up to the recent movements, would be of this ilk.

Eph. 4:11-13 The prophet is one of the five ministry gifts that Christ Jesus gave unto the Church for the perfecting of the saints and for the maturation of His Church.

Mk. 4:11; Eph. 3:5, Rev. 10:7 God reveals by His Spirit the mysteries of His eternal purposes in the Church to His apostles and **prophets.**

Eph. 4:11-13 PROPHETS are among the BUILDING AND INSTRUCTIVE ministries which are given as a gift of Christ to the Church for the **perfecting (maturing)** of His Church from **infancy** to **childhood** to **adolescence** to **adulthood.**

The Church cannot become fully mature without prophets.

Prophets must continue to function in the Church until the Church is fully mature.

APOSTLES and PROPHETS are **SPIRITUAL FOSTER PARENTS** to the Church, laboring on behalf of Christ to spiritually rear believers, developing them unto full maturity unto the measure of the stature of the fullness of Christ. **1 Cor. 4:14-17**: As an **APOSTLE** to the Corinthians, Paul addressed them as **"my beloved children"**, and said he had **"become"** their **"FATHER through the gospel."**

Eph. 3:3-10 Apostles and **PROPHETS** are channels of spiritual **revelation.**

The entire New Testament revelation — **THE MYSTERY OF CHRIST** — was **revealed** to **APOSTLES** and **PROPHETS.**

A Biblical Perspective of the Prophetic Gifts and Office

So also, **full illumination** of and **divine understanding** for the application of the Word, Wisdom, and Will of God often times comes through the ministry of the **APOSTLES** and **PROPHETS** today.

Amos 3:7 As in the Old Testament dispensation, God still reveals His **secret counsel** unto His servants the **PROPHETS** in the New Testament Age.

Eph. 3:5, Rev. 10:7 In the New Testament dispensation, God reveals by His Spirit the mysteries of His eternal purposes in the Church to His apostles and **prophets.**

(Much more on the Ministry of Prophets in a later section.)

LESSON 7
THE PARTICIPATION OF PROPHETS
IN THE PLANS OF GOD THROUGHOUT THE AGES
(Part IV)

PROPHETS PARTICIPATE IN ALL OF GOD'S PLANS AND PERFORMANCES.

AT THE END OF THE CHURCH AGE AND IN THE FINAL JUDGMENT

>**Prophets** are mentioned eight (8) times in the final end-time events in the Book of Revelation.

>**Rev. 11:3-13** Prophets will also be **instruments** of God **to execute His judgments** at the end of the Church Age.

>**Rev. 11:3,10** The infamous **"TWO WITNESSES"**, God's special envoys who **prophesy** (speak on behalf of God) during the last three and one-half years of the Tribulation period prior to the final judgment, could, according to one theory, symbolize the ministry of the company of **APOSTLES AND PROPHETS** who have been restored in the last days, operating in the spirit and power of **Elijah** and **Moses**.

>>Since God does not operate by reincarnation, it would be highly improbable that these two witnesses would actually be Elijah and Moses themselves.

>>**v. 4; cf. Zech. 4:1-14** Two olive trees = two lampstands = anointed ones. These verses and the two "anointed ones" represented in the verses correspond to one another in typifying Moses and Elijah.

>>**vv. 5,6** "And if anyone desires to harm them, fire proceeds out of their mouth and devours their enemies" — **cf. 2 Kgs. 1:9-12**. "These have the power to shut up the sky, in order that rain may not fall during the days of their prophesying" — **cf. 2 Kgs. 17:1-19:41-45; Jas. 5:17, 18**. All of this speaks symbolically of the ministry of **ELIJAH**.

>>**v. 6** "and they have power over the waters to turn them into blood, and to smite the earth with every plague, as often as they desire" — alludes to the ministry of **MOSES**.

>>**Lk. 9:27-32** Mt. of Transfiguration event — the Son of Man coming in His Kingdom — appears with **Elijah** (type of **prophets**) and **Moses** (type of **apostles**).

>>**(v.7)** It is interesting to note that the devil will be powerless to harm or hinder their ministry until "they have **finished their testimony**."

These **prophets** are **instruments** of God to **execute His judgments**, which provides evidence that there are **"JUDGMENT PROPHETS"** among the different types of prophets that exist. The judgment prophets will soon be emerging.

A Biblical Perspective of the Prophetic Gifts and Office

Rev. 16:6 The third bowl of wrath from God turns the water tributaries on Earth to **blood,** avenging the blood of martyred saints and **prophets**.

Rev. 18:20,24 **Prophets** are personally addressed by God during the final judgment and fall of Babylon.

Rev. 22:6 "the God of the spirits of the **prophets**."

Rev. 22:8,9 The **angel** (one of the seven angels with the bowls of wrath **[21:9]**) who acted as John's guide in Paradise and showed him things God ordained him to see, said of himself that he was "a **fellow-servant** of **yours** and of your brethren the **prophets**." Thus, we see that the very Hosts of heaven, who abide in strict obeisance unto God Himself, not only explicitly acknowledge the *existence* of prophets right to the end of the age, but also reveal that there are certain angels assigned to *serve* apostles (John) and the prophets in particular.

SECTION III:

THE ESTABLISHMENT OF THE PROPHET IN THE CHURCH

LESSON 8
THE SHADOW: THE ASCENSION OF ELIJAH

2 Kings 2:1-15 ELIJAH ASCENDS — ELISHA INHERITS HIS ANOINTING

1 Cor. 10:11 These things (Old Testament events) were written for our example and our instruction. The Old Testament is more than just history; it is really **"His Story."** The events of the Old Testament are not fictional fables given to us merely to provide good Sunday School material, rather they are types and shadows of that which would be fulfilled under the New Testament.

The story of Elijah was a foreshadow of **Christ** and the **Church**: **Elijah** is a foreshadow of Christ and **Elisha** is a type of the Church.

2 Kgs. 2:1-6 As we pick up the story, Elijah, knowing that the Lord is about to take him up, tells his protégé, Elisha, to stay in Gilgal, while he departed on his farewell tour to the cities where the schools of prophets were, Bethel and Jericho. Elijah was the senior prophet of Israel and had been tutoring the "sons of the prophets" (prophets in training) in these schools.

> But, Elisha, who had been Elijah's personal servant and student for quite some time, refused to stay behind. So together they journeyed to each city. At each city, the sons of the prophets there said to Elisha, "Do you know that the Lord will take away your master from over you today?" Each time, Elisha responded that he did indeed know it, and for them to be quiet. And, at each city, Elijah again told Elisha to stay behind, but he refused.

2 Kgs. 2:7 This verse may indicate why it was that Elisha was chosen to inherit Elijah's anointing rather than any of the other prophets in that they all "stood **opposite** them **at a distance**, while the two of them stood by the Jordan." Analogously, many fellow Fivefold ministers stand opposite (oppose) at a distance, distancing themselves from their fellow servants, the prophets, out of fear, intimidation, misunderstanding, misinformation, misguidance, or jealousy, or a combination thereof.

> Elisha had been willing to walk where Elijah walked over the years that he served Elijah. Many people want the anointing some men of God have, but they are not willing to pay the price and to walk where those men have walked in order to get that anointing. Elisha was; he had faithfully stood by Elijah's side for years. Elisha had not been looking for notoriety, fame, or glory, but was willing to be a servant and a student, to such a degree that he was known as the one "who used to pour water on the hands of Elijah" **(2 Kgs. 3:11)**, which according to the customs of the day was supposed to have been the menial chore of women.

> "...the two of them stood by the **Jordan**." The Jordan river was no pristine, babbling mountain-brook. It was filthy and full of pollution. A step into the Jordan was a step into degradation (cf. the story of Naaman **[2 Kgs. 5:1-14]**). Though it did not represent the official geographical boundary of Israel, it was the boundary of the Promise Land, "the land flowing with milk and honey." It was at the Jordan that Elijah's ministry

A Biblical Perspective of the Prophetic Gifts and Office

ended, and it was along the Jordan that John the Baptist ministered. Jesus said John the Baptist was Elijah who was to come. It is almost as though Elijah walked into the Jordan and John the Baptist walked out of it in the spirit and power of Elijah **(Lk. 1:17)** some 880 years later.

2 Kgs. 2:8 Besides being filthy, the Jordan was also too deep to cross where the two prophets stood, making this a real spectacle of suspense for the sons of the prophets who had followed to see what would happen. Elijah struck the waters of the Jordan with his mantle and they were supernaturally divided, and Elijah and Elisha crossed over on a divinely paved pathway of dry ground. Not so much as their little toe was contaminated by the filthy flow of the Jordan.

Elijah's anointing of power was contained in his mantle. His mantle was to him as Moses' staff was to him.

2 Kgs. 2:9 After they crossed the Jordan, Elijah asked Elisha what he could do for him before he departed. To some Elijah would seem to be rather arrogant to ask what he could do for Elisha before he left, and that would be flaunting his power. But that was truly insignificant compared to the audacity Elisha displayed by his response, which was to ask for a **"double portion"** of Elijah's anointing. In so doing, Elisha was in essence saying, "Elijah, I know you are a great man of God, a true prophet of God; and I have seen your power and your greatness for these many years I have served you; but I am not intimidated by your greatness, nor do I believe your ministry was the ultimate in what God can do; so I'm asking for a double measure of the anointing to be upon me that was upon you."

2 Kgs. 2:10 Elijah replies, "You have asked a **hard thing**. Nevertheless, if you see me when I am taken from you, it shall be so for you; but if not, it shall not be so."

Elijah knew what a **"hard thing"** it indeed was that Elisha was asking. Elijah said it was a "hard thing" certainly not in terms of God's ability to fulfill it, but in terms of what having such a great measure of the anointing would cost Elisha. Contrary to what some people think, having the anointing in great measure does not come cheaply, but rather at great personal cost to the recipient. Jesus had the anointing "without measure," and it cost him dearly in what he had to suffer on account of it. That is why so few people have the anointing in great measure, because they are not willing to pay the price it takes to have it. Many of those few through the ages who have had great measures of the anointing often had paid a great personal price for it.

Speaking by inspiration from God right until the very end of his ministry, Elijah told Elisha that if he was going to be a candidate for an anointing of that great of a measure, he was surely going to have to demonstrate his faithfulness right to the very end—he would have to be right there when God came to take Elijah, physically close enough to see him being taken up. If Elisha saw him when he was being taken up, then he would be granted his request. If not, then it would not be granted.

2 Kgs. 2:11 Then, as they were walking along together and talking, a chariot of fire with horses of fire separated the two of them and took Elijah up into heaven by a whirlwind.

2 Kgs. 2:12 "And Elisha **SAW** it...."

We are not told if the chariot of fire and the horses of fire were perceivable to the natural eyes when they came. We are not told whether or not the fifty sons of the prophets who stood on the opposite side of the Jordan saw the chariot and the horses. But in this verse there seems to be an especial allusion to the fact that Elisha **"SAW"** this supernatural event, an otherwise unnecessary allusion if it had been perceivable to everyone. A chariot of fire and horses of fire swooping up Elijah and departing by a whirlwind up into heaven would be rather difficult to miss if it were perceivable in the natural by natural sight.

It may be that when Elijah told Elisha earlier that he would know he had been granted his request if he **"saw"** him when he was being taken from him, that he was referring to Elisha being given the supernatural ability to see into the spirit realm and thereby see him being taken, and that that would be a sign to him that the anointing he asked for had come upon him.

Giving more credence to this possibility is the fact that Elisha later demonstrated that he had indeed received this supernatural ability to see into the spirit realm. In an ensuing incident, Elisha was able to perceive the angelic army of God which surrounded him and the city of Dothan as protection against the king of Aram though they were not manifest to the sight of others, that is until Elisha prayed that the Lord would enable his servant to also see the angelic army **(2 Kgs. 6:8-17)**, afterwhich his servant also did indeed see them.

Ability to "see" things supernaturally is a trait of prophets. In fact, it was because of this ability that prophets were originally called "seers" **(1 Sam. 9:9)**. Now, in the New Testament dispensation, an identifying characteristic of true prophets is that they are proficient in at least two of the revelatory gifts as well as the utterance gifts of the Spirit.

This ability to see into the spirit realm by this greatly anointed prophet and others for whom he prayed is the type and shadow of the manifestation gift of the Spirit of the "discerning of spirits," one of the revelation gifts. There is no such a thing as "the gift of discernment," as some erroneously think; rather it is the "discerning of **spirits**," which means precisely what it says, it is the supernatural ability to perceive the presence of **spirits**. There are four categories of spirits: 1) Divine (the Spirit of God); 2) angels; 3) demonic (the fallen angels); 4) human. Through the operation of the discerning of spirits one can perceive the presence of spirit-beings by supernatural sight into the spirit world.

Regardless, we know that Elisha did indeed receive the double-portion anointing he asked for because the Bible records exactly **double** the miracles performed by Elisha compared to Elijah.

2 Kgs. 2:13,14 As Elijah was taken up, his **mantle fell to the ground** — this is the most significant part of this entire event (as we shall see in a moment).

Mantles and the anointing are not needed in Heaven, where Elijah was going. They are needed here on Earth. The anointing is given as a channel for the manifestation of the power of God unto others. Elijah's ministry was over; he did not take his anointing into Heaven with him, but it was left behind unto his successor, Elisha.

"Where is the Lord, the God of Elijah?" Elisha took the mantle of Elijah and went straight to the place at the Jordan where he and Elijah had crossed over earlier. Elisha knew that God was no respecter of persons—the same God who had worked for Elijah would also work for him.

"And when he had also struck the waters, they were divided here and there; and Elisha crossed over." Elisha took the mantle of Elijah and struck the waters of the Jordan with it just as Elijah had done moments earlier. After all the years of tutoring under Elijah, Elisha had learned well not to be timid when it came to wielding the power of God. He didn't just "pat" the water, hoping that something would happen. He **"struck"** the waters, demanding that they part as they had for Elijah. And, sure enough, they did, and Elisha returned back over the Jordan on dry ground just as he and Elijah had crossed over together previously.

This was the first miracle Elisha performed—there was no sense in waiting around— either he had received the double-portion anointing he had asked for or he hadn't, so he boldly put it to the test, and, lo and behold, the mantle worked for him just like it had worked for Elijah!

2 Kgs. 2:15 "The spirit of Elijah rests on Elisha." The baton had now passed to Elisha, so to speak, and the anointing that had been upon Elijah was tangibly upon Elisha, only it rested on Elisha in double measure of what it had been upon Elijah.

LESSON 9
THE FULFILLMENT: THE ASCENSION OF CHRIST
(PART I)

As mentioned in the previous lesson, the Old Testament story of the ascension of Elijah into Heaven was a foreshadow of the ascension of Christ Himself into Heaven. As such, it contains two segments of symbolism regarding the Church which are fulfilled in the New Testament dispensation.

In this lesson we will deal with the first segment of symbolism, which is the representation of the establishment of the prophet in the Church. As we examine the truth found in the symbolism of this story, remember that in the story of Elijah and Elisha, as stated in the preceding lesson, Elijah symbolized Christ and Elisha represented the Church.

2 Kgs. 2:15 "The spirit of Elijah rests on Elisha."

>The story of Elijah's ascension into heaven and the relegation of his anointing unto Elisha is symbolic of the establishment of the **PROPHET** (along with the other Fivefold ministries) within the Church.

>When Elijah ascended, his mantle, which contained his anointing of divine power, fell to the ground. Elisha picked it up and went to the place at the Jordan where he and Elijah had crossed over on dry ground moments earlier after Elijah had caused the waters to be divided asunder by striking the waters with his folded mantle. Then, Elisha cried out, "Where is the God of Elijah," and struck the waters as Elijah had done. The waters were again divided in two, just as they had been for Elijah, and Elisha crossed the Jordan on dry ground.

>When the sons of the prophets saw what had happened they said, "The spirit of Elijah rests on Elisha." In other words, the prophetic mantle of power which had rested upon Elijah and which demonstrated that he was the premier prophet of Israel had now been transferred or relegated to Elisha. Elisha was now the senior prophet of Israel. None of the other prophets had as powerful an anointing as did Elijah, and now that anointing of preeminent power rested upon Elisha.

>In fact, as they would see, that mantle would produce double the miracles in the life and ministry of Elisha as it had for Elijah. Elisha did indeed receive the "double-portion" anointing he requested—the Bible records exactly **double** the miracles performed by Elisha as compared to Elijah.

Eph. 4:7-11 New Testament Fulfillment

>By revelation of the Spirit the Apostle Paul reveals what really took place on the Day of Ascension as Christ ascended into Heaven to sit down at the right hand of the Father, having completed His priestly ministry and mission of redemption. We know Paul's knowledge of this matter was by way of revelation because he himself was not there on the Mt. of Ascension on the Day of Ascension to witness Christ's ascension as were the twelve Apostles of the Lamb. This was only a fragment of the vast wealth of supernatural revelation the great

Apostle Paul received, which he neither received from men nor was taught, but which he received "through a **revelation** of Jesus Christ" **(Gal. 1:11,12)**. This is a stellar example of the previously **concealed** mysteries of Christ which are **revealed** through God's holy apostles and prophets in the Spirit" **(Eph. 3:1-5)**.

It is extremely interesting that this revelation was given to us by the Apostle Paul, who was not there on the Day of Ascension, rather than by one of the Apostles of the Lamb who were eye-witnesses of Christ's ascension. Those who witnessed this incredible occurrence first hand were no doubt awestruck by what their eyes saw. Apparently, they were so captivated by the awesomeness of what they saw happening right in front of their own eyes in the natural that not one of them perceived what was taking place in the spirit realm. Apparently, not one of them saw what the Apostle Paul saw taking place during Christ's ascension when it was revealed to him by the Spirit. All too often, our spiritual vision is similarly impaired by what we see through our physical eyes. Perhaps it required someone who had not been an eye-witness to the pomp and circumstance of the magnificent event to tell us what all happened in the spirit realm as Christ ascended to take His seat of Sovereignty at the right hand of the Father.

By revelation of the Spirit the Apostle Paul reveals that when the resurrected and glorified Christ was ascending into Heaven **(Acts 1:9)**, after having fully completed His Divine assignment of redemption for all of mankind, in similar manner as Elijah's mantle had fallen to the earth upon his departure, so also Christ's mantle of anointing fell down upon His hand-picked successors. Jesus had chosen these men to be His successors following His departure. He had said to them, "As the Father has sent Me (the Supreme Apostle), so send I you (subordinate apostles)."

v. 4 ONE Body of Christ. "**Now** are **YOU** Christ's body, and individually members of it" **(1 Cor. 12:27)**. When Christ ascended into Heaven and sat down at the right hand of the Father, symbolizing that His work on Earth was finished, the Church of His followers became the Body of Christ on Earth.

v. 7 "But to **EACH ONE** of us **GRACE (GIFTINGS)** was given according to the measure of **CHRIST'S GIFT**."

Each member of the Body of Christ has been given "charis," that is, "giftings." Peter essentially echoed this statement and adds an exhortation for every believer, therefore to utilize or employ the gift he or she has been given **(1 Pet. 4:10)**.

This verse coupled with the preceding verses points out that every believer has a calling and has been given giftings to fulfill that calling. The "gifts" referred to in this verse must of necessity be those found in **Romans 12:6-8**, known as the motivation gifts (of necessity, because this is the only grouping of giftings of which every believer is given one). Every believer is given one of these gifts, which gift is the one gift that primarily motivates the believer. Verse four of this same chapter of Romans also indicates that though there is only one Body of Christ, all the members comprising the Body do not have the same function. Verse six echoes what was spoken in the above cited passages, that though they differ, we all have been given gifts.

"according to the measure of Christ's gift"—the giftings we are all given are given, astonishingly enough, in the measure in which Christ Himself possesses them, which is limitless; albeit, probably no believer has ever been able to operate the gifting he has been given according to its full potential.

v. 8 "**Therefore**, it says, **WHEN HE ASCENDED ON HIGH...HE GAVE GIFTS TO MEN.**"

When Jesus ascended into Heaven, as the mantle of Elijah did not go up with him, but remained, so also Jesus did not take the giftings which He possessed and operated while here on planet Earth where they are needed with Him into Heaven. These giftings were intended to be a blessing to needy mankind here on Earth. Thus, when Jesus ascended into Heaven, He relegated His giftings unto men and women in His Body here on Earth.

1 Cor. 12:4-6 Three different groups of giftings, each emanating from and given by a different Member of the Trinity:

v. 4 "varieties of **gifts**, but the same **SPIRIT**": refers to the **MANIFESTATION** gifts (aka, "the Charismatic Gifts") which are given by **God the SPIRIT, the HOLY SPIRIT**, delineated in **1 Cor. 12:7-11**:

Revelation Gifts
1. Word of Wisdom
2. Word of Knowledge
3. Discerning of Spirits

Power Gifts
4. Faith
5. Gifts of Healings
6. Working of Miracles

Prophetic Gifts
7. Unknown Tongues
8. Interpretation of Tongues
9. Prophecy

v. 5 "varieties of **ministries**, and the same **LORD**": refers to the **MINISTRY** gifts which emanate from and are given by, **God the SON**, Jesus as the Head of the Church to minister on His behalf as His personal envoys, delineated in **Eph. 4:11**:

1. **Apostles**
2. **Prophets**
3. **Evangelists**
4. **Pastors**
5. **Teachers**

v. 6 "varieties of **operations** (workings) [translation of Greek word is "energizings"], but the same God who works (operates, energizes) all things in all persons" — refers to the **MOTIVATION** gifts, which are bestowed by **God the FATHER**, delineated in **Rom. 12:6-8**:

1. **Prophecy**
2. **Serving**
3. **Teaching**
4. **Exhortation**
5. **Giving**
6. **Governing**
7. **Showing of Mercy**

v. 11 Here, Paul delineates the **MINISTRY GIFTS** which Christ gave or relegated unto certain believers, which are also commonly referred to as the "Fivefold Ministry Gifts": Apostles, **Prophets,** Evangelists, Pastors and Teachers. It was as Jesus was ascending into Heaven that He relegated these ministry gifts unto the Church. Thus, the Church Age began with **ALL** of the Ministry Gifts in activation.

In the case of Elijah during the Old Testament dispensation, the mantle of the prophet had passed from Elijah to Elisha. But, in the case of Christ and the Church, His mantle was disseminated in the expanded form of the **MINISTRY GIFTS.**

"Some" — not "all." Only "some" believers are given a ministry office anointing, those chosen by the Lord Himself as the Head of the Church. While there is a priesthood or ministry of the believer, that ministry is **UNTO GOD** (see Acts 13:2; Rev. 1:6), which **ALL** believers are to operate in, there is another priesthood, a ministry reserved for and relegated unto ONLY Fivefold ministers, which is a priesthood to minister **UNTO THE PEOPLE** on behalf of Christ the Head.

> **Plp. 1:1** There are **three classifications** of function in the Body of Christ: **saints, overseers** (ministers), **deacons** (delegated servants).

> **Mat. 23:8 (L.B.)** "You are all **on the same level** as brothers." This speaks of "spiritual equality" among believers. We are indeed all on the same level spiritually speaking, "as brothers," because we all have the same Heavenly (i.e., spiritual) Father, and Jesus is our Big Brother. We all are seated with Christ at the right hand of the Father **(Eph. 2:6)**. We are all "**joint**-heirs" with Jesus Christ **(Eph. 3:6)**; none of us are "**junior**-heirs." There are no second class citizens in the Kingdom of God. There is no "big me, little you."

> **Rom. 12:4** However, there are differences among believers in terms of **function** and responsibilities. **EVERY saint** is given a **motivation** gift; **ANY** believer can be used as a conduit for the **manifestation** gifts as the Spirit distributes and wills; but only **SOME** are given Fivefold **ministry** giftings.

The Charismatic Move was a genuine move of God, the purpose of which was to restore the "charismata" or manifestation gifts into function in the Church. But, unfortunately, as in the case of every move of God, some error was also mixed in with the truth that God was restoring. In the Charismatic Move we heard over and over again the slogan, "We are **ALL** ministers." That, of course, is true in the sense that we are all able to minister as "ambassadors of Christ" to win the lost unto Christ and to be channels of the supernatural power of God via the manifestation gifts of the Spirit. Nevertheless, this does not in any way mean that we are **all** in **Fivefold** ministry. This verse clearly tells us that only **"SOME"** are appointed unto that anointing. The manifestation gifts are for every believer, but that in no way negates the necessity of governmental authority within the Body of Christ, which is the function of Fivefold Ministry Officers in the Army of God.

The Charismatic Move was a move to restore the gifts of the **HOLY SPIRIT** within the Church; the next move will be a move to restore the gifts of **JESUS** the Head of the Church and governmental authority back into the Church. The Charismatic Move restored **POWER** in a time of relative spiritual peace. In the next move, the Church will be transformed into "an exceedingly great army" of the Lord for a time of great spiritual conflict, and it will be **ORDER** that is restored.

A Biblical Perspective of the Prophetic Gifts and Office

LESSON 10
THE FULFILLMENT: THE ASCENSION OF CHRIST
(PART II)

The second segment of symbolism in the story of Elijah's ascension into Heaven is the representation of the Elijah anointing and the double-portion Elisha anointing that will come upon the Body of Christ at the end of the Church Age.

THE ELIJAH ANOINTING

With the restoration of the ministry of prophets back into their rightful place of function in the Body of Christ is coming an **ELIJAH** anointing upon the Body of Christ. The Elijah Company of End-Time Prophets God is raising up will bring the **purging** and **purification**, and the **restoration** and **refining** within the Church which is required in order for it to become that Church without spot or wrinkle which Jesus is coming back to claim for Himself, the Church that God will glorify.

It was Elijah who spearheaded the showdown on Mt. Carmel between himself as representative of the true prophets of the one and only true God, Jehovah, and the false prophets of Baal. In like manner shall the Elijah Company of Prophets spearhead the showdown of the ages between the people of God and the false prophets of the New Age Babylon False Church in the coming days. The God who answers by **fire** will be proven to be the only true God.

Elijah typifies **"Prophets of Power"** and the end-time **"Judgment Prophets"** the Lord will raise up in the coming days. These issues will be addressed in much greater depth in other sections of this course, but suffice it to say here that this end-time company of prophets will be the ultimate fulfillment of the last two verses in the Old Testament:

"Behold, I am going to send you Elijah the prophet (immediately) before the great and terrible day of the Lord. **And he (Elijah) will RESTORE..." (Mal. 4:5, 6).**

This verse tells us that God is going to send Elijah the prophet immediately before the day in which He releases His full wrath and vengeance upon the unbelieving world. The "Elijah the prophet" He sends just before "the great and terrible day of the Lord" will bring restoration. Malachi's prophecy came more than 400 years following Elijah's departure into Heaven. What did God mean by this prophetic mystery which closes out the Old Testament books? Surely God does not work by reincarnation—what, then, did He mean, when He said He would send Elijah the prophet?

It was the angel Gabriel that gave the answer to that question, which mystified the Jewish theologians for hundreds of years and which still mystifies Orthodox theologians of Judaism today. In announcing the birth of John the Baptist to Zechariah, Gabriel said, "And it is he (John) who will go (as a forerunner) before Him **IN THE SPIRIT AND THE POWER OF ELIJAH**, to turn the hearts of the fathers back to the children...." It was not that God was saying that Elijah himself would return, but rather that his **ministry** would be resurrected through another person, which in the case of the first coming of the Messiah was John the Baptist (cf. Mat. 11:14). However, John the Baptist was the Elijah who

A Biblical Perspective of the Prophetic Gifts and Office

would come to the **Jews** to make ready the Jewish people for the first coming of Christ **(Lk. 1:17)**. Again, Gabriel gave us insight into this matter: "And he (John) will turn back many of the **SONS OF ISRAEL** to the Lord their God" **(Lk. 1:16)**. John the Baptist's ministry was exclusively to the **Jews**, he was the Elijah sent to them — **the Jews**.

Mat. 17:11 "Elijah **IS** coming and **will RESTORE ALL THINGS**." It is critical to note that Jesus declared this **AFTER** the death of John the Baptist. Moreover, with the exception of restoring the hearts of some **Jews** back unto God through his message of repentance, John the Baptist restored **nothing**. Hence, for all these reasons, John the Baptist could not have been the "Elijah" of which Jesus was speaking. Rather, He spoke of yet another "Elijah" who would yet come, with a mission to "**restore all things**." That could only be "the restoration of **ALL** things about which God spoke through the mouth of His Holy prophets (e.g. Joel) from ancient times" **(Ac. 3:21)** — the restoration of all that was lost in the Church during the great deterioration of the Dark Ages, the restoration that has been ongoing ever since and will ultimately culminate in the full maturation of the Church-Bride "unto the measure of the stature of Christ" **(Eph. 4:13)**. While Jesus Himself was the literal, true "Elijah" of which He spoke, ever since the Day of Ascension, Jesus has been effecting this prophesied restoration within the Remnant Church He is building through His special surrogates, Fivefold ministers, unto whom He relegated His ministry anointing and authority during His ascension **(Eph. 4:7-12)**.

The **ELIJAH anointing** will result in the glorification of the Body of Christ here on planet Earth. We will then be "a people prepared" for the **SECOND COMING OF CHRIST**! But before He returns to set up His Kingdom reign upon the Earth, and before the Church is taken up to be with Christ, while the wrath of God is being poured out upon the unbelieving world, something else is going to take place — the entire corporate Body of Christ is going to receive the **ELISHA anointing**!

THE ELISHA ANOINTING IS COMING!!

2 Kgs. 2:15 "The spirit of Elijah rests on Elisha."

As we mentioned earlier, when the sons of the prophets saw the waters of the Jordan divided asunder as Elisha struck them, they realized that the mantle of power that had rested upon Elijah had now been passed on to Elisha. In fact that mantle which Elisha inherited from Elijah would produce double the miracles in the life and ministry of Elisha as it had for Elijah. The Bible records exactly **double** the miracles performed by Elisha as compared to Elijah, confirming the fact that Elisha did indeed receive the "double-portion" anointing he requested. But, what truth does this Old Testament type and shadow symbolize which will be fulfilled today in the Church Age?

Jn. 14:12 "Truly, truly, I say to you, he who believes in Me, the works that I do shall he do also; and **GREATER WORKS** than these shall he do; **because I go to the Father**."

There is an ELISHA ANOINTING coming upon the Body of Christ!

Following the **Elijah** anointing, when the Church has become **"glorifiable,"** will come the **ELISHA** anointing. The **ELISHA anointing** will be a **double-portion** anointing of the Spirit which shall be released upon the Church collectively and upon certain believers. This will be a time in which great signs and wonders shall be wrought through, not just

A Biblical Perspective of the Prophetic Gifts and Office

Fivefold ministers, but also many lay-believers. Multitudes shall be healed from every disease known to mankind, including leprosy, cancer, AIDS, and every other incurable disease. Many who are blind and deaf shall see and hear. Some who have been made lame and halt by crippling diseases, paraplegics, and the severely handicapped shall receive creative miracles to cure their deficiencies. A number of the insane and mentally impaired shall be delivered. Great numbers will be saved. And, there will be numerous cases of the dead being raised. Ordinary believers shall be walking in malls, airports, and other public places, and their shadow alone shall bring healing to unsuspecting passersby, without so much as even a conscious prayer.

The entire world shall take note of the end-time Church; it shall indeed be "a **glorious Church** without spot or wrinkle, washed in the blood of the Lamb!" For a brief time the eyes of the world shall be upon the exaltation of a people, a people who once were not a people, but who are now **THE PEOPLE OF GOD!**

"Where is the Lord, the God of Elijah?"

Many people today are beginning to echo the cry of Elisha, **"Where is the Lord, the God of Elijah?"** In other words, "Where is the God of demonstration of the Spirit and Power?" They are crying out to see the **demonstration of the power of God in our midst** as it was in the days of Elijah and Elisha.

A ground-swell is rising in the rank and file of the Church. Many people have grown weary of "business as usual" in the churches. They are now saying, "We want to see the power of God manifested in our midst that we have heard you preachers preach about for all these years. Where is it?" The true Gospel does not come in **WORD ONLY**, but also with power in the Spirit unto full conviction **(1 Thes. 1:5)**. With many churches, it's talk, talk, talk, words, words, words, with very little demonstration of the power of God. Multitudes of believers have grown extremely weary of that spiritual impotence.

A SPIRITUAL REVOLUTION IS COMING!

1 Cor. 15:46 First comes the natural, then the spiritual. What takes place in the natural is often a preview of what is about to take place in the spirit realm. The populace revolts that in the mid to late '80's began taking place around the world in many different countries against the oppressive regimes which had ruled over them with an "iron fist" for so long is a reflection of the spiritual revolution that is about to take place in the Church.

A **spiritual revolution** of sorts is on the horizon, in which the people of God will begin to clamor for men and women of God who will stand up as Elijahs and Elishas and be bold enough to believe God for the **double-portion anointing**. The circumstances that will be facing everyone in the days ahead will require strong, bold spiritual leaders to lead the people of God into battle against the forces of the enemy. The days that lie ahead will be no time for wimps! What we need is Elijahs and Elishas—men and women of power and boldness!

A CHANGING OF THE GUARD IS COMING!

God is indeed now beginning to raise up these Elijahs and Elishas—a **"NEW BREED"** of leader—men and women of power and boldness, who cannot be bought off by greed, compromised by the politics of men, or side-tracked by the temptations of the devil. They will be leaders who refuse to be man-pleasers, but strive only to please God. They will not be afraid to bring reproof, reform, and even rebuke where necessary to whomever regardless of their status and personal cost. Many will be sovereignly raised up by God out of total obscurity.

A changing of the guard is about to take place in leadership in Christendom. Many well-known leaders will soon begin to be replaced. Some will go on to be with the Lord, having faithfully completed their course and assignment, having been used mightily of the Lord in making great contributions during former restorational movements. Others will transition into a new role as "senior advisors" behind the scenes, assisting the new leadership out of the wealth of wisdom they have accumulated over their years of conflict. Still others who resist the move of God and the changing of the guard will be sovereignly removed by the Lord.

This changing of the guard will be likened unto the passing of the scepter of Israel from Saul unto David. Saul served his purpose. But, Saul himself was only a **"subject"** of God; he never did have a heart after God as did David. Saul was full of stubbornness and selfish-ambition. He often disobeyed God and even when he did obey it was out of duty and not out of a heart that was toward God. "If you be willing and obedient, you will eat of the good of the land," Isaiah said **(Is. 1:19)**. Saul, like many today, was not willing even when he *was* obedient, and often, though *mentally* willing, he could not find enough will to be obedient in *deed*. Because Saul was only a **subject** of God himself, he reproduced **subjects**, and his mentality caused him to reign with domination and control over those who he "**subjected**" unto himself.

Not so with David. David was a man "after God's own heart." Though his flesh at times gave him as much trouble as it does all of us, his heart was full of the attributes of God's heart. David's heart was a heart of willingness rather than stubbornness, obedience rather than selfish rebellion. Saul was overbearing, dominating, manipulative, and controlling, and reigned with an iron-fisted authoritarianism. David, on the other hand, was full of true humility, respect, and preference for others, and he retained his kingship through the **esteem** he engendered, not through heavy-handed **authority**. David was not a mere "**subject**" of God, but his heart was the heart of a true "**servant**" of God. Thus, David in turn produced **servants**. His leaders were fiercely loyal servants of David because David proved himself to be a true servant of God and man. Yet, though David was indeed a meek servant, his monarchial authority was in no wise diminished by his meekness.

The new breed of leaders God is raising up will be "**Davids**" not "**Sauls**." They themselves are true servants of both God and man. They will not demand that others be subjugated under them, but will govern with full authority by way of the **esteem** by which they will be honored by others. They will lead through servitude. They will not build kingdoms and thrones of monarchial reign for themselves, but will honor Jesus as the King of Kings and Lord of Lords, and expend their efforts and energies exclusively toward building His Kingdom in the lives of believers.

Jesus was the ultimate Servant of the Lord, and He said even He did not come to be served but rather to serve. He taught that the greatest leaders in the Kingdom of God are those that will truly be servants, who are given great respect by others because they greatly respect others, preferring others in honor (Rom. 12:10). Jesus harshly rebuked the hypocritical scribes and Pharisees for constantly doing things to vaunt themselves above others, and said, "But the greatest among you shall be your servant. And whoever exalts himself shall be humbled and whoever humbles himself shall be exalted" (Mat. 23:1-12).

LESSON 11
THE VALIDITY OF THE PROPHETIC OFFICE IN THE NEW TESTAMENT CHURCH

HEB. 1:1,2 THE OFFICE OF THE PROPHET WAS NOT ABOLISHED by the coming of Christ and His enactment of the New Testament, but rather **WAS THEREBY FURTHER ESTABLISHED,** so that **GOD NOW SPEAKS *"IN HIS SON"*** (NASB) **JESUS** (The Manifested Messiah), not *OF* the Messiah about whom the Old Testament prophets spoke as the Messiah who was yet to come.

This passage of Scripture has been used by some as a supposed proof-text for the theory that the office of the Prophet is not a valid ministry office in the New Testament Church. However, the import of this passage not only does **not** invalidate the ministry office of the Prophet, but actually provides further proof of its *ESTABLISHMENT* in the New Testament Church.

The true import of this passage is that the Old Testament prophets spoke on behalf of God **OF** the coming Messiah, i.e., the **SON**. However, now that Jesus has come and enacted the New Testament, prophets in the New Testament age speak on behalf of God **IN** the **SON**. To state it more succinctly:

Old Testament prophets spoke (foretold) *OF* the Messiah who was to come, whereas, New Testament prophets speak on behalf of God *IN* Christ,.

In other words, Old Testament prophets spoke from **external** inspiration of the Spirit; New Testament prophets speak from **internal** inspiration of the indwelling Spirit of Christ. The Spirit of Prophecy now released within believers is the "testimony of Jesus" spoken through believers **(Rev. 19:10)**.

HEB. 9:15-17 Jesus was the **TESTATOR** of the New Covenant.

Eph. 1:10 Everything pertaining to God, godliness, and eternal life is **"SUMMED UP IN CHRIST."** I.E., the sum of the New Testament message **IS** Jesus!

MAT. 5:17 The substance of the Old Testament was **FULFILLED (ABSORBED)** by Christ, **NOT ABOLISHED (DONE AWAY WITH).**

All of the Old Testament was **"ABSORBED"** (not abolished) in Christ—He was the embodiment of all that was spoken in the Law and the Prophets.

Heb. 7:18,19; 8:6-13 The only thing from the Old Testament that was **abolished** was the means by which we were to gain rightstanding with God, which was now by grace through faith in Christ, rather than through the ordinances of sacrifices (See **Rom. 3:21-26; 5:1**). It was the **WAY** unto rightstanding with God that was abolished from the Old Testament in the New Testament. Jesus had now become the only true and valid **WAY** unto God. "I am the **WAY**...," He said. So in this sense, what was abolished by the New Testament events was our **GUILTINESS** for our sins. Jesus **remitted** our sins, that is to say, He totally purged, or

A Biblical Perspective of the Prophetic Gifts and Office

wiped them out, so that they literally no longer exist, whereas, under the old covenant they were merely "**covered over**" until the coming of the Messiah.

The New Testament brought forth an abrogation of the Old Testament **TYPES AND SHADOWS (Heb. 8:5)**, because the Person whom they typified had now come. Jesus **WAS** the true sacrificial Lamb that was slain before the foundations of the world as the propitiation of our sins.

The Old Covenant certainly was not lies or only partial truth as the theology of some regarding Old Testament truths seem to imply for "God is not a man that He should (lit., can) lie" **(Num. 23:19)**. God did not change from the Old Testament to the New. What He was in the Old Testament, He still is in the New Testament dispensation:

"For I, the Lord, **do not change**" **(Mal. 3:6)**.

"Jesus Christ is **the same** yesterday, **TODAY**, and forever" **(Heb. 13:8)**.

Jesus did not **ABOLISH** the substance of the Old Covenant, but rather He **ESTABLISHED** it as the **FOUNDATION** of the New Testament, and it was **FULFILLED** by Christ.

"There's a line that's drawn through the ages, And on that line stood an old rugged cross..."

Everything of the Old Testament passed **THROUGH CHRIST ON THE CROSS** into the New Testament; thereby, the Old Testament was fulfilled in Christ, and became the foundation of the New Testament. Thus, the Old Covenant is **established** by the New, and was then further expanded by the New. In effect, the New Testament is an **"amplification"** of the Old Testament.

1 COR. 12:27 NOW that Christ Jesus has ascended into Heaven and sat down at the right hand of God, **WE**, the many-membered Church of true believers in Christ are the manifestation of the Body of the Messiah on Earth.

1 Cor. 12:12-31 Since Christ Jesus ascended into Heaven, the Body of Christ is now a many-membered Body here on Earth, which has been anointed and equipped to vicariously complete the ministry of Jesus unto the mankind for whom He died to bring redemption.

EPH. 1:22, 5:23 CHRIST is the functional **HEAD** of the Church.

One of the greatest problems in Christiandom today is a misunderstanding regarding the matter of governmental authority. Many leaders have thought that leaders of churches are a part of the "headship" within the Church. We have heard much talk of this matter of "headship" with the Body in terms of governmental authority within the local church. Yet, that may very well be the gist of the problem. The Bible says that Jesus Christ is the only **GOVERNMENTAL HEAD** of the Church. He has bought and paid for the Church with His own shed blood. He is the only One deserving of that position. The truth of the matter is that Jesus is not the true functional Head of many churches and religious organizations. Because He is not physically here in the flesh, human leaders have usurpingly imposed themselves into, and are occupying, His rightful place as Head in most church organizations. In fact, many churches even cast a vote as to who is going to be their head. But, the true place of Headship is not vacant, and never has been since the Church began. The Apostles of the Lamb, after Jesus' ascension in Heaven, were themselves keenly aware that Jesus Himself was the true functional Head of the Church. Of course, they had lived with Him for three and a half years prior to His departure. If only we today could have that same sense about His literal Headship of the Church, and that we, leaders and laymen alike, are all members of His Body, i.e., His servants sent to carry out His purposes, plans, and pleasure.

Is. 9:6 The **GOVERNMENT** of the Kingdom of God, which is now operating through the Church, is on **CHRIST'S SHOULDERS**. Who are the *shoulders* of the Body?

Deut. 10:8; 1 Chron. 15:15 The **LEVITES** carried the Ark of God's Presence on their *SHOULDERS*. During the Old Covenant, spiritual authority rested with the Levites. Thus, the shoulders in the Body of Christ are the **Levites**, which in the New Testament era are the "**Local Church Presbytery**," or elders. Biblically, "elders" are Fivefold ministers.

1 Cor. 12:28 This verse delineates the offices that comprise the "Local Church Presbytery." These "elders" or "overseers" are the Levites within the local church, set in by God to govern the matters of that local assembly (1 Tim. 3:1,4,5; 5:17). Local governing and ministering elders are the New Testament counterparts to, the fulfillment of the type and shadow of, the Old Testament Levites. All New Testament "Elders" must be those who have been anointed and appointed by God with Fivefold ministry giftings **(1 Tim. 3:1,2)**.

The following would summarize all this:

HEAD = SOVEREIGNTY = JESUS HIMSELF

The **BODY (CHURCH) = SERVANTS = BELIEVERS (Leaders and Laymen)**

The part of the Body upon which His **GOVERNMENT** rests is His **SHOULDERS; thus:**

SHOULDERS = LEVITES = LOCAL CHURCH PRESBYTERY = ELDERS

In the human anatomy, the **SHOULDERS** are a part of the body, and are the part of the body upon which the **HEAD** rests. This is significant, because it is the same way in the Body of Christ—the **shoulders** are a part of the Body in that they too are human-beings who are believers in Christ and thus have been baptized by the Spirit into this many-membered Body of Christ. Thus, all of the **MINISTRY OFFICES** are a part of the New Testament Body of Christ.

RESULT: The result of everything we have discussed thus far in this lesson is that the **OFFICE OF PROPHET PASSED THROUGH THE CROSS OF CHRIST** from the Old Testament Age into the New Testament Church Age, and was further established and given a higher level of authority to operate—*IN* the Son.

Under the Old Testament, the only ministry office operable was the office of the prophet, which is precisely the point of Heb. 1:1. Under the New Testament, however, the **office of prophet** was **established** and **embodied** by Jesus when He came, and was then in fact expanded or disseminated into four additional offices by Christ when He ascended on High. So, in essence, we see then that all the other Fivefold ministry offices emanate from the Old Testament **office of the prophet**.

SECTION III: THE ESTABLISHMENT OF THE PROPHET IN THE CHURCH

Mat. 11:9,10 In fact, in John the Baptist, we see the beginning of the Fivefold ministry dissemination. John was declared by Jesus to be a **PROPHET**. Yet, He then declared Him to be the first New Testament **APOSTLE**, even before the original Apostles of the Lamb, when He declared that John was also **"ONE WHO IS MORE THAN A PROPHET"**—**"MY MESSENGER" (V.10)**, which is precisely the characterization of what an **APOSTLE** is—a "special messenger" or spokesman (prophet) sent out by God with a special message. **An apostle is a prophet who is more than a prophet—a prophet sent out with a special message and mission.**

1 COR. 12:28 Apostles and **PROPHETS** have been **SET (PERMANENTLY APPOINTED)** in the Church as foundational ministries by God Himself (cf., Eph. 3:10).

Notice that this passage indicates that it was God Himself who set these ministries into the Church. And, there is absolutely no evidence in Scripture that He has ever rescinded those appointments. The term **"SET"** used by the Holy Spirit in this text expressly alludes to the permanence of the appointment of these offices within the Church. Anyone who has every worked with cement knows very well what the word "set" means—you must work very quickly to place it precisely where and how you want it, for once the mixture has "set," it is permanently fixed. The same is true of the ministry gifts—they are a **permanent** fixture within the Church for the duration of the Church Age. Apostles and prophets are valid New Testament ministries as long as the Church and the Church Age exist.

No where does Scripture explicitly state or even imply that any of the ministry gifts have been **dispensationally depleted,** or cemented into a non-functional foundation or abolished. Rather, they have always been **(Lk. 1:70)** and will always be vitally active and functioning throughout God's eternal plan of the Ages.

Heb. 13:8 Jesus Christ (including the Body of Christ) is **the same** yesterday, today, and forever. What Jesus has ever been, He still is, and ever will be. God changes not **(Mal. 3:6)**! Jesus is still the High Apostle, the Premier Prophet, the most Eminent Evangelist, the Chief Shepherd, and the Master Teacher. Thus, Apostles and Prophets, as well as Evangelists, Pastors, and Teachers still exist today, because Jesus still exists, and He has relegated all that He was and is unto the Church **(1 Jn. 4:17)** to complete His mission and ministry here on the Earth.

Eph. 4:11-13 **ALL** the ministry gifts will continue to function toward the perfecting and edifying of the Church—**"UNTIL"**—we **ALL** attain unto **the unity of the faith and of the knowledge of the Son of God (UNITY OF DOCTRINE)** and full **MATURITY**. When the Church-Bride reaches full maturity, Jesus will return to claim her as His Eternal Companion. The Church Age will culminate with the Marriage Supper of the Lamb. Until then, we shall remain in the Church Age. We are still in the Church Age. Thus, all the ministry gifts are still necessary, needed, and therefore, still functioning.

This verse delineates the offices comprising the **"local church ministry presbytery,"** or the governing elders.

> Elders govern; and elders are men who have been appointed and anointed by God to function as Fivefold officers **(1 Tim. 5:17)**. True elders are never mere laymen. Those appointed by God into these offices are the men who have been given the responsibil-

ity to govern and manage the matters concerning the operation of the local church. They are the **"Levites"** unto the local church. Their authority, however, is limited to that particular local church into which they have been set by God.

One major problem in the Body of Christ today is a lack of revelation regarding the matter of governmental authority in accordance with the letter and spirit of Scripture. The revelation is in the Bible, but few understand it. Then to add to the problem, the "Discipleship Movement" brought forth into prominence much error in this regard.

Governing authority is not "universal," but is limited to the group into which a minister is set as a governing elder. Universal governing authority in the Church-at-large does not exist, nor is there any valid "authority structure" among Fivefold ministers. Jesus made all this clear in telling the Apostles lording over one another **"is not so AMONG YOU" (Mk. 10:35-45)**. Governing authority is only necessary in the local church. There is no purpose or use for authority among Fivefold ministers at-large. For instance, apostles do not rule over prophets, or prophets over evangelists. It simply does not work that way. Relationships among Fivefold ministers are based upon "esteem" not "authority." Some Fivefold ministers choose voluntarily to establish relationships with other ministers for mutual accountability and ministry one to another as a matter of prudence. Such relationships must be established by **choice** not by **coercion**.

Eph. 2:20 The ministry of the **APOSTLES AND PROPHETS** is the very **FOUNDATION** of the Church. They are the ministries upon which the entire Church structure rests.

Eph. 4:11-13 Apostles and Prophets are among the **BUILDING AND INSTRUCTIVE** ministry gifts and offices.

1 Cor. 3:10,11 Apostles and Prophets are **MASTER BUILDERS** (Spiritual General Contractors) & **FOUNDATION LAYERS**. The apostles and prophets are the chief builders of the House of the Lord, the Church. Jesus Himself is the foundation **(1 Cor. 3:11)** which is laid by the chief builders. The **apostle** is the **"master builder"** (which today would be called the "general contractor") and the prophet is the **chief architect** who supplies the blueprint of revelation **(1 Cor. 3:10)**.

Hag. 1:1 Apostles and prophets represented in this prophetic word regarding the rebuilding of the "house of the Lord."

The Divinely-inspired message containing the blueprint of revelation is given through the **PROPHET** Haggai.

Zerubbabel is the **governor** of Judah. The New Testament counterpart of the Old Testament office of governor or king is the office of the **APOSTLE**.

Joshua was the **high priest** in office at the time. The Hebrew name **"Joshua"** is translated **"Jesus"** in the New Testament language, Greek. Jesus Christ is the true High Priest **(Heb. 3:1)** of which the Old Testament high priests were symbolic. Joshua the high priest is represented here as the "cornerstone" of this triumvirate.

Thus, we have represented in this verse: **Apostles** and **Prophets**, who were under the spiritual auspices of the **High Priest**. These were given the charge to rebuild the house of the Lord. Compare this verse with its New Testament counterpart, **Eph. 2:20**, which states: (God's Household,) having been built upon the foundation of the **APOSTLES** and **PROPHETS**, **Christ Jesus Himself** being the **CORNERSTONE**.

EPH. 3:3-10 THE REVELATION MYSTERY OF CHRIST IS REVEALED TO THE APOSTLES & PROPHETS IN THE SPIRIT

The revelation of Christ comprising the **New Testament** was revealed to **APOSTLES & PROPHETS** by supernatural revelation by the Spirit. (See Paul's example—**Gal. 1:11,12**)

2 Pet. 1:19-21 ALL the New Testament was written by APOSTLES & PROPHETS through inspiration of the Spirit (**2 Tim. 3:16**).

Thus, **full illumination** of the Word, Wisdom, and Will of God will come through the ministry of the **APOSTLES & PROPHETS**—**Eph. 3:9,10.** They will not write a new Bible, but will bring further **ILLUMINATION AND REVELATION of the specifics** given to us in the 66 Books of the Bible in order to better understand and properly apply the Logos Word of God which has already been given to us.

Amos 3:7 God reveals His **secret counsel** through **PROPHETS**. There is secret counsel in the heart of God that He will reveal only through His servants the prophets. How much easier it would be to build the work of the Lord, if leaders would consult the prophets for secret counsel from the heart of God.

SECTION IV:

DETERIORATION AND RESTORATION IN THE CHURCH

LESSON 12
THE DEMISE OF THE MINISTRY GIFTS

INTRODUCTION In the last section we examined the establishment of the prophet, as well as the other Fivefold ministry offices within the Church. We also established the fact that the Church Age began with all the Fivefold ministry offices in operation, and that they were all intended by God to be functioning throughout the duration of the Church Age. Unfortunately, however, according to history, that is not at all what transpired. The account of what did happen is of vital importance in order to understand clearly why a move of God to restore the ministry of the Prophet (as well as the Apostle) into its rightful place of function within the Church became necessary. Without the backdrop of Church history, it is difficult to fully understand the significance of the "times of refreshing" and "periods of restoration" which have transpired over the last four hundred and eighty years in order to bring restoration of what was lost in the Church less than three hundred years after its inception. The intent of this section is to put this matter of the demise and restoration of the ministry gifts into its proper perspective within the framework of Church history. Thus, it is only a very simplistic overview of Church history that is presented. For students desiring a more comprehensive study of the subject of Church history, many volumes are readily available in bookstores and libraries.

BIRTH OF THE CHURCH There are several schools of thought regarding the birth of the Church. Some say it was born on the Day of Pentecost. Others argue that since Jesus was the "first-born of many brethren," He was, thus, the first member of the Church, and therefore the inception of the Church was the birth of Jesus. Still others contend that the Church began on Easter morning when Jesus rose from the dead, thereby becoming "the first-born from the dead" and the first member of the Church. Still others point to Jesus' Baptism in the Spirit as the day the Church was born, and some even say the Church was born when Jesus entered the upper room and breathed upon the disciples to impart the Holy Spirit to them following His resurrection and priestly ascension. None of those theories is without merit. Yet, more important than the Church's nativity is the fact that it was indeed born in power and that it was born with all of the ministry giftings of Jesus in operation.

INFANCY OF THE CHURCH Most theologians do agree that the Church's period of "infancy" began sometime around 30 A.D. and lasted to about 100 A.D. During this period, the Church is often referred to as "the Early Church." The growth of the Church and the record of supernatural events occurring during the Church's infancy is phenomenal and truly amazing. History bears out that the number of those associating themselves with the Church in Jerusalem grew from the one hundred and twenty which congregated in the upper room to several hundred thousand within the first year alone. Moreover, though the early disciples did not launch out from the Jerusalem Church to begin fulfilling the "Great Commission" of Christ to evangelize the Gentile nations until they were forced to do so by the great persecution which arose in connection with the martyring of Stephen, within the first forty years of the Church's existence, the Gospel apparently, according to the Apostle Paul, had been preached "unto every creature under heaven" **(Col. 1:23)**.

This is significant in that there is much to-do made today about the return of Christ being contingent upon "the preaching of the Gospel to every nation and tribe," and so on, especially by those who with vested interest extol the importance of modern media such as television as a primary

A Biblical Perspective of the Prophetic Gifts and Office

vehicle for the fulfillment of that prerequisite. Yet, if the chief contingency for the return of Christ was merely the dissemination of the Gospel to every tribe and nation, then Christ would have surely returned around 62 A.D. when Paul wrote in the Colossian Epistle that the Gospel had already been preached to "every creature under Heaven," that is to say, ostensibly—to every person alive at that time.

POWER, BUT NOT PERFECTION The Book of Acts records the plethora of supernatural events that took place in the early days of the Church through the early Apostles. It gives us a record of God's performance of the promise He gave to the disciples at the outset of the Book— that when the Holy Ghost came upon them, they would be endued with supernatural power by which they would be His witnesses "in Jerusalem, and in all Judea and Samaria, and even to the remotest part of the earth" (Ac. 1:8). This record gives us more than ample evidence that the Early Church indeed possessed great **POWER**.

Nevertheless, Christ did not return to claim the Early Church as His Bride. Why not? The answer is that something else was yet required in order for the Church to be the Bride suitable unto Christ. What could have been lacking? Though the Early Church did indeed possess a measure of **power** for service, and though that power enabled the early disciples to be powerful witnesses of the resurrected Christ unto the entire world, it was **not** the power she manifested that would make the Church-Bride suitable unto Christ. The prerequisite for eternal communion of Christ and the Church is not **power**, but **PERFECTION**, that is to say—**MATURITY**.

Eph. 4:7-13 This passage indicates that the Church Age will culminate with the eternal marriage of Christ to His Church-Bride when the Body of Christ has become **ONE "MATURE MAN"** (one, united, completed, fully matured Body), unto the full measure of Christ Himself. It is only then, that the Church will be a suitable Bride for Christ, when she is "**in all her GLORY**, having no spot or wrinkle or any such thing; but...holy and blameless" (Eph. 5:27). It is then, when the Church has been glorified, that Christ will return to claim the Church as His eternal Bride.

Ac. 3:21 This verse also indicates that Christ cannot return until the Church has reached full maturity. It explicitly states that Heaven must **RETAIN** Christ until "all things about which God spoke through the mouth of His holy **prophets** from ancient times" are totally restored during all the divinely appointed "periods of restoration" which have and will yet take place. Christ will not return one "nano-second" before the full maturation of the Church and until the complete restoration of all things that shall be restored within the Church has taken place through the Apostles and Prophets. Neither Israel, nor events in the nations of the world, are the weather-vane to watch to decipher the imminence of Christ's return, but rather—the **CHURCH**! Christ is not coming back to claim a country in the Middle East, i.e., *natural* Israel, as His Eternal Bride, but rather, *spiritual* Israel, i.e., the Church—"a chosen race, a royal priesthood, a **HOLY NATION**, a **PEOPLE FOR GOD'S OWN POSSESSION**" (**1 Pet. 2:9**)!

FORCED WEANING FROM JUDAISM—DESTRUCTION OF JERUSALEM—70 A.D.

Mat. 5:17 Jesus was the fulfillment of the Old Testament. He was what all the types and shadows of the Old Testament represented. He was the mediator of a New Covenant **(Heb. 12:24)**. His appearance and the redemption He purchased with His shed blood rendered the Old Covenant ordinances as the **way** unto rightstanding with God **null and void**. The New Covenant in Christ's blood superseded the Old Covenant and made it forever obsolete. When He came, Jesus plainly declared, "I am **THE WAY**, the Truth, and the Life, no man can come unto the Father, except by Me." Jesus Christ inaugurated **"a new and living way"** of access into the Holy Place of fellowship with God through the veil of His fleshly vicarious death. The ceremonies and rituals of **Judaism** were no longer "the way" but rather **Jesus** was now **the only WAY**. Since Jesus was the fulfillment of the types and shadows of the Old Covenant, Judaism with its rituals and observances was no longer necessary, and thus became **obsolete** with the coming of Jesus **(Heb. 8:6-13)**.

Nevertheless, the Early Church refused to break it's ties with the customs and rituals of Judaism for forty years after the ascension of Christ. The Jewish Church as a whole just could not get themselves to fully disassociate their faith in Christ for salvation from the ancient traditions of the religion of their forefathers, though it was now as "unauthorized" as the false religions of Rome, Greece, and Babylon.

Many today who receive the Lord Jesus Christ as their Savior also are not able to fully separate their faith in Christ from the rituals and observances of the religion in which they have been reared. Such is the case with some contemporary so-called Messianic-Jewish believers, who while professing faith in Christ as the Messiah, also continue to practice Judaistic liturgies and rituals in so-called "New Testament Judaism" churches. The Truth is that there is no such a thing as "New Testament Judaism." Such groups are nothing more than modern-day Galatian Churches, with the same unfortunate result that they "have been severed from Christ...seeking to be justified by the (Jewish) law; and...have fallen from grace" **(Gal. 5:4)**. In a similar way, some Catholics, Lutherans, and Episcopalians professing faith in Christ, continue to practice unScriptural rituals and observances, recite unScriptural creeds and liturgies, and to adhere to unScriptural doctrines after being Born Again and receiving the Baptism in the Spirit. This is error. True believers are to "come out from among them and be separate," and assemble together with an element of the one and only true Church, which God's Word tells us is comprised of both Jews and Gentiles.

Therefore, because the Early Church refused to obey God's charge to disengage themselves from the traditions of Judaism in order to worship the Lord in Spirit and in Truth, the Lord Himself, in order to demonstrate the utter obsolescence of Judaism, divinely orchestrated the virtual annihilation of the city of Jerusalem along with the most sacred icon of Judaism — Solomon's Temple. On August 10, 70 A.D., the Roman Army under the command of General Titus attacked and invaded Jerusalem, pillaging, plundering, and destroying. The devastation was complete: Josephus calculated that 1,100,000 Jews were killed in the city; another 257,660 were killed in surrounding areas; and 97,000 other Jews were taken captive. Even Titus acknowledged divine assistance in bringing destruction to Jerusalem: **"We have fought with God on our side; and it is God who pulled the Jews out of these strongholds: for what could machines or the hands of men avail against such towers as these?"**
YET, NOT ONE CHRISTIAN PERISHED in the destruction of the city of David, because unlike the disbelieving Jews, the Church heeded Jesus' warning: **"But when you see Jerusalem surrounded by armies, then recognize that her desolation is at hand. Then let those who are in Judea flee to the mountains, and let those who are in the midst of the city depart...because these are DAYS OF VENGEANCE, in order that all things which are written may be fulfilled"** (Lk. 21:20,21).

The Temple caught on fire and burned to the ground. The heat was so intense that the gold and other precious metals melted and ran in between the blocks of the foundation. The soldiers disassembled the temple stone by stone to retrieve the gold and precious metals, fulfilling Jesus' prophecy concerning the Temple — **Mat. 24:1,2**. With the destruction of the City of David and the Temple of Solomon, God resoundingly reiterated that His official

Headquarters and place of habitation was no longer in the Law and Tabernacle of Moses, or in Solomon's Temple, and not even in Jerusalem, but was now in the **CHURCH**. With this annihilation of the last remaining icon of Judaism, God's intent was to obliterate the last remaining vestige in the minds of all Jewish believers henceforth of reliance upon the rituals of Judaism as the means of gaining rightstanding with God.

GREAT PERSECUTION: 90 A.D. to 313 A.D.

Following the destruction of Jerusalem, the Church began to undergo years of persecution. The previous persecutions were a result of divine discipline, the goal of which was to force the early disciples to obey God's commands and thereby carry out His plans and purposes for the promulgation of the Gospel in all the world. The continuous years of persecution that started around 90 A.D., however, unlike the previous few intermittent persecutions and including the destruction of Jerusalem, was authored by Satan, the Church's arch-adversary **(1 Pet. 5:8)**, in an attempt to destroy the Church. These persecutions were examples of occasions in which the wrath of the wicked is poured out against the righteous **(1 Tim. 3:12)**. This was the kind of suffering—"according to the will of God"—that the Apostle Peter was alluding to in his letter addressed to those believers who were residing "as aliens, scattered (by the persecution) throughout Pontus, Galatia, Cappadocia, Asia, and Bithynia," to whom he wrote this exhortation: "Therefore, let those also who **SUFFER ACCORDING TO THE WILL OF GOD** entrust their souls to a faithful Creator in doing what is right" **(1 Pet. 4:19)**.

Persecution's Purposes. The persecution of the Church served to keep it **purified** and **purged** of hypocritical, deceptive, dishonest, and insincere tares for nearly 300 years. It kept the chaff separated from the wheat in that becoming a Christian meant possible loss of citizenship, imprisonment, occupational repercussions, monetary deprivation, torture, possible crucifixion, burning at the stake, being made public sport of by being thrown to wild animals, abduction, sexual and physical abuse of the young women, enslavement, and other heinous treatment.

Christianity Outlawed. Eventually, on the basis that it was a threat to Roman customs, laws, mercantile mores, polytheism, and the social class system, Christianity was actually outlawed during the era of the Great Persecution, and all Christians were stripped of their rights of citizenship within the Roman Empire.

DETERIORATION: 313 A.D.—Dark Ages

The Great Persecution of the Church ended with **Emperor Constantine's Edict of Toleration** in 313 A.D., which sanctioned Christianity and outlawed persecution of Christians. Constantine favored Christians and encouraged all his constituents to convert to Christianity as their religion simply by way of declaration rather than by virtue of a true Born Again experience.
The Church had passed through periods of **preservation** to periods of **persecution** and now had come to a period of **political prosperity.**

Seventy years after Constantine's Edict Of Toleration, **Emperor Theodosius** took it a step further and actually made Christianity **compulsory** and the **official state religion** of the Roman Empire. This was the final blow against any remaining hope for the preservation of Truth and purity by the Church. With this imperial act, the Church had begun its **darkest hour**, what became known as—**THE DARK AGES**.

A Biblical Perspective of the Prophetic Gifts and Office

1 Tim. 4:1,2 "But the Spirit explicitly says that **in later times some will FALL AWAY FROM THE FAITH,** paying attention to **deceitful spirits and doctrines of demons,** by means of the hypocrisy of liars seared in their own conscience as with a branding iron."

This was the Great Apostasy for the corporate Church, concerning which the Apostle Paul prophesied. During this age of spiritual darkness, the Truth was subverted by humanistic ideologies and vain philosophies — the doctrines of demons of which Paul forewarned **(cf. Col. 2:8)**. Eventually, nearly all the foundational teachings and doctrines of the Church were distorted, perverted, diluted, invalidated, or totally abandoned.

One of the primary causes of this horrendous spiritual debacle was the fact that the Bible was taken out of the hands of the saints. Common believers were prohibited from reading the Bible and eventually from even possessing one, on the basis that uneducated commoners were not qualified to rightly divide and interpret Scripture; that was a task for which only the academically educated theologians were fit. Only these Roman Catholic clerics were allowed to read, study, and interpret Scripture. Theologians whose theology was based more and more on the unScriptural, humanistic writings of the medieval European philosophers, told the people what to believe and established their own humanly-conceived and unScriptural doctrines, many of which are still the premise for doctrines espoused today in some mainline denominations. As a result, the light of personal spiritual illumination soon grew extremely faint, and eventually great darkness prevailed over the Church, for **it is the entrance of the Word of God that gives light or illumination (Ps. 119:130)**.

By now the Roman Catholic (Universal) Church was the only sanctioned religion of the Roman Empire. It was officially part and parcel of the Empire. Since they were usually the most highly educated, clerics often held the highest political posts. As a whole, Roman Catholic clerics had become an elite corp of corrupt empirical statesmen and officials bent on malevolent domination of the plebian common folk.

Jesus' apocalyptic admonition to two of the Asia Minor churches some two-hundred years before this time plainly conveys His utter disdain for the premise of such ecclesiastic hierarchical sovereignty over the saints. He *commended* the Ephesian church saying, "Yet this you do have (in your favor), that you hate the deeds of the **Nicolaitans, WHICH I ALSO HATE.**" On this score, He *condemned* the Pergamum church, however, saying, "I have a few things against you," among which one charge was that some among them "hold the teaching of the Nicolaitans," which He follows with this solemn command: "Repent therefore; or else I am coming to you quickly and **I will make war against them** with the sword of My mouth." The components of the term *"Nicolaitans"* ("nico" = to conquer; "laitans" = laity) combine to convey the thought of: "those who conquer the laity." The Nicolaitans were the beginning of what became the elite corp of Roman Catholic clergymen. (It is interesting to note that the term "priest" was not used as an attribution to the clergy until after the Second Century as the Nicolaitan doctrines became more widespread.)

The **early Church leaders** sought to heed Jesus' teaching that the greatest among them were to be **servants of all,** and were not to **"lord it over"** the flock of God. But as the Spirit of Christ diminished in the Church, the desire for **prestige, prominence,** and **power** by the clergy increased. **SERVITUDE** was soon supplanted by **SELF-AGGRANDIZEMENT** among clergymen in the Church.

A Biblical Perspective of the Prophetic Gifts and Office

The Church Age began with the ministry offices of apostles, prophets, evangelists, pastors, and teachers in operation. These men were the overseers and elders who provided shepherdship and oversight to the Flock of God. Early church ministers were men who had responded to a solemn calling and responsibility; they were not seeking a position, prestige, prominence, or power.

Unfortunately, however, the **Pharisee Spirit (Mat. 28)**, which has always plagued the Church, was never completely purged from the Early Church. Consequently, the **Ministry Offices & Gifts were** eventually **abrogated** and replaced by a **religious hierarchy** (the papal system of bishops and a pope) through which the clergy "lorded over" the people. The Nicolaitan clerics craved dominance and control. Their strategy was to subjugate the people of God under them for their own selfish gain. Jesus emphatically declared that He hated their demonically inspired teaching and their deeds **(Rev. 2:6)**.

Some of the other major departures from the Truth occurring during this time which contributed to the deterioration of the Church were: the replacement of simplistic and spontaneous worship in the Spirit, the only true worship **(Jn. 4:23,24)**, by formalistic liturgy ("holding to a form of godliness, but denying the power thereof" **[2 Tim. 3:5]**); conversion of pagan customs into Christian rituals and observances; the institution of the practice of penance; the integration of religious icons as objects of devotion and other religious paraphernalia as supposed aids in worship; the veneration of Mary; and, the canonization of departed saints.

Although there were a few sparks of would-be reform during the Dark Ages, each was eventually extinguished, and for 1,200 years the Church languished in its **CORPORATE "Great Apostasy."**

LESSON 13
THE RESTORATION

JOEL 1:4; 2:23-25   DETERIORATION FORETOLD

The deterioration of the Church discussed in the previous lesson was foretold by the Prophet Joel possibly 1,200 years before it commenced. Though Joel's prophecy foretold of events involving the Jewish nation which indeed came to pass, its greatest import was the foretelling of the progressive deterioration of the Church. On the Day of Pentecost, Peter stated categorically that a portion of Joel's prophecy had its initial fulfillment in the outpouring of the Spirit which occurred on that Day **(Acts 2:16-21)**.

As evidenced by the brief account in the previous lesson, the spiritual devastation which occurred during the Dark Ages all but extinguished the candle of illumination in the Church. During its genesis, the Seed of Truth, the essence of Christ, had truly been planted in the good soil of obedient believers comprising the Early Spiritual Church. As it was watered by the Jesus-appointed and -anointed Fivefold ministers to whom He had imparted His ministry giftings, the Seed of Truth continued to produce generation after generation of spiritual harvests of Born Again fruit. Maturation and reproduction of the Heavenly hybrid continued as long as the garden in which the Seed of Truth had been planted was watered by Spirit-inspired teaching, and as long as it remained purged of the poisonous *weeds* of false doctrines, as well as the *tares* of false believers. But, when the purging of persecution ceased, and the Fivefold gardeners of God were supplanted by the humanistic clerics of the Structural Church, the garden soon became overrun by weeds and tares, and the flow of Heavenly water ceased. Ultimately, this caused the Heavenly hybrid to dry up and be choked out, and to return to its form as a Seed buried in the ground, where it lay dormant for 1,200 years.

JOEL 2:18-29   RESTORATION FORETOLD

If Joel's prophecy concerning the deterioration of the Spiritual Church had been all that he prophesied, the Seed of Truth would have remained buried forever. Fortunately, however, Joel also prophesied God's promise of ensuing restoration.

vv. 18,19 The Lord pledges that at some point following the deterioration He will once again become zealous for the Church, will have pity on His people and will answer their prayers, sending them **grain** (The Word of God), **new wine** (Revelation), and **oil** (Anointing) in satisfying measure, and further pledges that He will never again allow the Church to be displayed as a complete reproach before the nations.

vv. 20,21 The Lord pledges to bring about the debacle of the Roman Empire—"because it has done great (terrible) things," and God tells the Church not to fear, for He, the **Lord** Himself, also "has done great things."

v. 22 **Beasts of the field** (ostracized reformers, pioneering preachers) encouraged because the **pastures of the wilderness** (the outcast true spiritual church) have turned green (indicating new life, revitalization), for **the tree** (Cross of Christ, Tree of Eternal Life) has borne fruit (believers), **the fig tree** (natural Israel, progenitor of the Church) and **the vine** (Spiritual

A Biblical Perspective of the Prophetic Gifts and Office

Israel, the Church) has born its fruit.

v. 23 God exhorts the **Sons of Zion** (Born Again Believers) to rejoice and be glad in the Lord because He has given the Church both the **early rain** which produced the initial harvest period of the first 300 years and the **latter rain** of "the times of restoration" which has been producing the last day harvest.

v. 24 The threshing floors (true spiritual churches that are bringing forth the whole counsel of the Word of God and allowing it to separate the wheat from the chaff, the spirit from the flesh) will be full of **grain [wheat]** (the Rhema Word of God) and the **vats** (vessels; ministers of the Word) will be overflowing with **new wine** (fresh revelation from God) and **oil** (anointing, power).

v. 25 Following the Dark Ages, God pledges to make up to the Sons of Zion for the years of spiritual devastation and suppression which occurred under the domination of the Medieval tyrannical empires.

v. 28, 29 Another outpouring of the Spirit is promised **"after this"**—the Dark Ages—the greatest fulfillment of which indeed began to happen around the turn of this century.

ACTS 3:17-21 TIMES (PERIODS) OF RESTITUTION (RESTORATION)

Just as the deterioration of the Church was prophesied by the Prophet Joel, so also the subsequent "times of restoration" were also prophesied by the Apostle Peter only days after the Day of Pentecost. Surely, the inspired words he spoke must have been puzzling to the Apostle, but they were proven to be accurate some 1,500 years later, and still stand yet today as a divinely inspired prophecy from God.

v. 17 The contemporary religious rulers and leaders of Peter's day acted in ignorance of all that God was doing. They had their minds so fixed upon their own religious activities that they totally missed the plan of God as it was being unveiled right before their eyes. The same is true yet today of the vast majority of church leaders and lay-believers—they are so intent on "playing church" and acting out their preconceived roles that they totally miss the true plan and purposes of God for the Church being revealed right now by the Lord Himself. Remember, this is the same Peter that Jesus rebuked sometime before, saying, "Get behind Me, Satan; for you are not setting your mind on God's interests, but man's." (Mk. 8:33)

In order to be able to comprehend what "God's interests" are, it is vital that we understand this matter of spiritual restoration God has been effecting since the Dark Ages. Like the blind man who Jesus healed (Mk. 8:23-25), many only "see **MEN** as trees walking around," as a result of His first touch. Many need a second touch from the hand of Jesus in order that they may see **GOD** and what **HE** is doing rather than only what **MEN** are doing supposedly on His behalf. Most ministers and believers alike are guilty of setting their minds on man's interests in all their activities which they purport to be doing all on behalf of and in the Name of the Lord. Many today, especially in the sophisticated structural churches of western "civilization" need to be anointed with eye-salve by God in order to begin to see from God's perspective instead of merely from the human perspective. The only way to accurately appraise all that is happening throughout the world is to see it from the perspective of God, from the vantage point of the Church, for the sum total of all that is taking place in the entire cosmos is the exaltation of a people, the people of God, the Bride of Christ, the Church.

The highest purpose of all that God has been doing since and including the Creation of the world is the bringing forth of a holy race of people who would be worthy of eternal fellowship with Him and eternal communion with His Son Jesus Christ. Paul E. Billheimer in His classic masterpiece on the subject of the centrality of the Church-Bride in the purposes of God, *Destined For The Throne*, capsulizes the Divine universal plan with these words of extreme profundity:

> "The human race was created in the image and likeness of God **for ONE purpose: TO PROVIDE AN ETERNAL COMPANION FOR THE SON**. After the fall and promise of redemption through the coming Messiah, the Messianic race (Israel) was born and nurtured in order to bring the Messiah. **And the Messiah came for ONE intent and only one: TO GIVE BIRTH TO HIS CHURCH, THUS TO OBTAIN HIS BRIDE**. The Church then—the called-out body of redeemed mankind—turns out to be the **CENTRAL OBJECT, THE GOAL,** not only of mundane history but **OF ALL THAT GOD HAS BEEN DOING IN ALL REALMS, FROM ALL ETERNITY**." (Paul E. Billheimer, *Destined For The Throne*, Fort Washington, PA, Christian Literature Crusade, 1975, p. 22.) [Capitalization and emphasis added by the author.]

"The letter kills, but the Spirit gives life" **(2 Cor. 3:6)**. There is a danger of getting so caught up in mental knowledge of the historical aspect of Christianity alone. It is the Spirit of God that gives us spiritual life and vitality, not the accumulation of mental knowledge regarding the things of God. Many theologians and theological students have a great deal of knowledge **about** God and theological matters in their minds, yet are without the vitalizing life and power of God in the heart. Christ is still a Person, not a theological subject. It is His power, the **ANOINTING**, that breaks the yoke, not **ACADEMICS**. Despite the plethora of volumes of sophisticated theological knowledge that have been compiled over the years by academical theologians and assimilated by students of theology, it is still nonetheless true that "the kingdom of God does not consist in **WORDS**, but in **POWER**" **(1 Cor. 4:20)**. When Jesus comes to measure the sum total of our lives at the Judgment Seat of Christ, He will not be grading us on the basis of how much academic knowledge we had accumulated over the course of our Christian life, but rather on how much of His Divine **POWER** we had attained and activated during our tenure on Earth.

Yet, God's power is contained in His Word **(Heb. 1:3)**—so, to assimilate His Word in your spirit is to attain unto His power. Thus, the other side of the coin is that we must also understand that God certainly places no premium on ignorance either. Ignorance is most definitely **NOT** bliss. "My people are destroyed for lack of knowledge (ignorance of God's Word)" **(Hos. 4:6)**, God says. Spiritual as well as Scriptural ignorance will destroy you. Accumulation of academic theological knowledge is not a requirement by God in terms of our relationship with him, but renewal of the mind **(Rom. 12:2; Eph. 4:23)** through assimilation of Spirit-inspired and Spirit-communicated knowledge—i.e., "the mind of Christ" **(1 Cor. 2)**—indeed is a Divine directive.

In order to understand what all God is doing in the Church today with the present restorational move, it is vital to view it on the screen of Church history. The restoration that started following the Dark Ages around the turn of the 16th Century is still continuing today as we approach the 21st Century. Comprehending what God **IS** now doing, is contingent upon our knowledge of what He **HAS** done as well as what He has **PROMISED** to do.

v. 18 Israel did not recognize their long-awaited Messiah when He finally came because they did not fully comprehend "the things which God announced beforehand by the mouth of all

A Biblical Perspective of the Prophetic Gifts and Office

the prophets," even when those things were being fulfilled right before their eyes. God always announces beforehand by His servants the prophets what He is about to do **(Amos 3:7)**.

v. 19 The process applicable in any age by which "a **time of refreshing** may come from the presence of the Lord" is delineated in this verse: **repent and return**. Notice that "time(s) of refreshing" come only from the presence of the **Lord**, not from the presence of **men**. Especially in the past few years, the Body of Christ has been "suffering" from over-exposure to the presence of **MEN**. Now, more than ever before, we need the **"presence of THE LORD"** to be manifest in the Church and in our services. When the "presence of the Lord" is manifest there is healing, miracles, deliverance, signs and wonders, prophetic utterance, and revelation, unending flow of God's love—all that mankind could ever need to be whole and content. This verse discloses the needed prerequisite which will allow the "presence of the Lord" to be manifested before us—**REPENT and RETURN**. In this century there has been "a time of refreshing" about every twenty years:

1907 - Azusa Street Movement
1927 - Pentecostal Movement
1947 - Healing Movement
1967 - Charismatic Movement
1987 - Prophetic Movement

v. 20 This verse indicates that when the Church begins to repent and return, Jesus, the Anointed One, will visit the Church with a supernatural manifestation of His power. All throughout Church history, when believers began to repent from their lukewarmness, apostasy, and worldliness, and began to return to the Lord, Jesus was manifested in a new and different way, a different form. He came as **"The Reformer"** during the Protestant Reformation, **"The Sanctifier"** during the Holiness Movement, **"The Baptizer in the Holy Spirit"** during the Pentecostal Movement, **"The Evangelist"** during the Healing Movement, and manifested Himself as **"The Pastor and Teacher"** during the Charismatic Movement, in which He reintroduced His Body to the ministry of the Holy Spirit. During this next move Jesus will be appearing as **"The Premier Prophet"** to manifest His glory by Personal visitation unto the churches. Some will receive Him in His ministry as the Prophet, some will reject Him. Out of ignorance, some will say this move is not of God—God will forgive their error because it is spoken out of ignorance. Yet, others will blatantly reject the revelation given to them by the Holy Spirit and cross the line to commit blasphemy against the Holy Spirit, becoming guilty of an eternal sin for which they will never receive forgiveness **(Mk. 3:22-30)**, by attributing the works of power manifested in this move to the devil, as did the Pharisees, who centuries earlier accused Jesus of casting out demons by the power of the devil.

v. 21 Heaven must **"retain"** Christ until "all things about which God spoke by the mouth of His holy prophets from ancient time" have been restored in the Church by means of all the divinely appointed and orchestrated **"periods of restoration."** The matter of the retention of Christ in Heaven "until..." corresponds to the "until" mentioned in verse thirteen of the Apostle Paul's dissertation regarding the ministry gifts continuing to function until the Church becomes "a (one) [fully] mature man, to the measure of the stature of the fullness of Christ" **(Eph. 4:7-13)**. The Fivefold ministry giftings of Christ which He has given to the Church for its maturation will continue to function until this ultimate objective is accomplished. When the final objective of the full maturation of the Church is accomplished the Church will be united with Christ for eternal communion and the effecting of the Marriage Supper of the Lamb. Thus, the only thing keeping Christ in Heaven is the maturation of the Church to become that glorious Church without spot or wrinkle **(Eph. 5:27)** for which He will return to claim her as His eternal Bride. The very purpose of "periods of restoration" is the progressive spiritual restoration and maturation of the Church to become that glorious Church.

THE GREAT RESTORATION OF THE CHURCH BEGINS: October 31, 1517 — The Protestant Reformation.

On the eve of All Saints Day, October 31, 1517, an agitated and disgusted Augustinian monk by the name of **Martin Luther** nailed a list of 95 theological arguments against the unScriptural practices of the Roman Catholic Church to the door of Castle Church in Wittenburg, Germany. Though this previously obscure priest had in no way intended his "**95 Theses**" to be a defiant call for **revolution,** but rather only an appeal for **reformation**, the Church, nevertheless, declared war against Luther and his followers because of his unCatholic, albeit Scriptural theological teachings.

Regardless of his own personal intentions, the spark generated by Luther's hammer as it struck the nail affixing his "95 Theses" to the door of the Church kindled fires of revolution and restoration which spread throughout the known world and continue to burn yet today. Entirely unbeknownst to him, God had chosen the formerly obedient cleric to spearhead the spiritual revolution historians termed **"THE PROTESTANT REFORMATION,"** which was the inception of the **"TIMES OF RESTORATION"** God had promised through His Prophets and the Apostle Peter **(Acts 3:21)** centuries earlier.

Since 1517 until today, nearly five-hundred years later, God has been restoring to the Church everything that was lost, supplanted, abrogated, and abandoned during the Dark Ages, progressively reestablishing the Church in "present truth" **(2 Pet. 1:12)**.

FOUR MAJOR RESTORATIONAL MOVEMENTS ("TIMES OF RESTORATION")

There have been **FOUR MAJOR RESTORATIONAL MOVEMENTS** since 1517, each of which resulted in the chronological restoration of one of the six major doctrines of the Church **(Heb. 6:1-3)**:

PERIOD	DOCTRINE RESTORED	RESTORATIONAL MOVEMENT
1500's	Repentance From Dead Works	Protestant
1800's	Faith Toward God	Holiness
1900's	Baptisms	Pentecostal
1950's	Laying on of Hands	Charismatic

THE LAST TWO DOCTRINES REMAINING TO BE RESTORED —

The Resurrection of the Dead (The Glorification of the Church)

The doctrine of the resurrection of the dead will be restored during the present **Prophetic Movement** which began in October, 1987 (exactly 470 years from the day Martin Luther nailed his "95 Thesis" to the door of the Church in Wittenburg). During this move of God, a company of prophets is being raised up and brought to the forefront within the Church in order to bring about the purification of the Church. The Church will undergo refining judgment during this period **(1 Pet. 4:17)**. The Prophetic Movement will not have a *culmination* as such but rather shall *crescendo* into a *coupling* with the next wave — the **Apostolic Movement** — in which many true apostles will be raised up as the apostolic ministry office is restored and reactivated. The main thrust of the Apostolic Movement will be the establishment of the order and government of the Kingdom of God in the lives of believers as well as in the churches. The siamese-twin Prophetic-Apostolic Movements will bring about the ultimate fulfillment of **Ezekiel 37** in which **"the valley of dry bones"** (the structural church) will be transformed into **"an exceedingly great ARMY."** It is the Lord Himself in His conversation with His prophet Ezekiel who equates this spiritual transformation with "the resurrection of the dead":

> "Then He said to me, 'Son of man, **these bones are the whole house of Israel [the Church];** behold, they say, "Our bones are dried up, and our hope has perished. We are completely cut off." Therefore **PROPHESY**, and say to them, "Thus says the Lord God, 'Behold, **I will open your graves and cause you to come up out of your graves, My people;** and I will bring you into the land of Israel. **Then** [during the resurrection of the dead restorational movement] **you** [the whole Church, both Gentiles and Jews] **will know that I am the Lord** [that Jesus is the Messiah], when I have opened your graves and caused you to come up out of your graves, My people. And I will put My Spirit within you, and you will come to life, and I will place you on your own land. Then you will know that I, the Lord, have spoken and done it,' declares the Lord.""" **(Ezk. 37:11-14)**

The restoration effected by the Prophetic-Apostolic Movement will result in the finishing purification and establishment of the Church necessary to make her worthy of and ready for glorification. As indicated in the above passage and in the verses that follow it, another important element of the restorational movement into which we have entered is that it will be during this period that the last day remnant of Jews recognizing Jesus as the Messiah **(Rom. 9:27, et al.)** will be manifested and "regrafted" onto the divine vine of the eternal family of God. (More on the subject of the coming restorational movement in Section V.)

Eternal Judgment (The Judgment of the Wicked)

> This period will involve the eternal judgment of the unbelieving of the world. Since "judgment begins with the household of God" **(1 Pet. 4:17)**, this period of judgment follows judgment of the Church effected in the former era.

THE RESTORATION OF THE MINISTRY GIFTS & OFFICES.

The Church Age began with **ALL** of the ministry gifts and offices in activation, but they were all subsequently nullified, deactivated, and totally abrogated during the Dark Ages as they were replaced by the ecclesiastical hierarchy of the universal Roman Church. During the last 50 years of the 20th Century, however, God began a process of **restoring** and **reactivating** **ALL** of the ministry gifts and offices with a particular emphasis each decade on one office:

APPROX. DECADE	OFFICE RESTORED	EMPHASIS OF MOVEMENT
1950's	Evangelist	(Healing & Deliverance Evangelism)
1960's	Pastor	(Restoration & Emphasis of Local Church)
1970's	Teacher	(Charismatic & Faith Teaching)
1980's	Prophet	(Purification, Illumination & Revelation)
1990's	Apostles	(Order, Maturity, Unity of Doctrine)

By the year 2,000, ALL THE MINISTRY GIFTS WILL BE REACTIVATED AND RESTORED TO OPERATION in the Church.

RESTORATION OF APOSTLES AND PROPHETS.

Most people are familiar with the ministry offices of: **Evangelist, Pastor,** and **Teacher.** However, by and large, the Church is not familiar with and is uninformed concerning the Ministry offices of: **Apostle and Prophet**. In this present restorational wave of the Spirit, God is bringing an **emphasis, activation,** and **magnification** of the **office of the prophet.** The next restorational wave will bring an emphasis, activation, and magnification of the office of the **apostle**.

True Prophets are now being raised up by God! God is bringing forth many Holy Ghost trained and anointed prophets out of their deserts of obscurity in order to finish the task of preparing the Bride for the return of the Bridegroom! These God-appointed Prophets will have impeccable motives devoid entirely of any shred of self-aggrandizement. The persecution which they have endured at the hands of the Pharisaical, religious-spirited structural church will have served its purpose of refining them as silver and gold in the fiery furnace of affliction, perfectly purifying their motives!

Section V:

the Coming Restoration and Purification

LESSON 14
RESTORATION AND REFORMATION

THE COMING FINAL TIDAL WAVE OF RESTORATION

The next great move of God's Spirit over this globe will be **a gigantic tidal wave** of unprecedented proportions. It will be **unrivaled** in all the annals of Church history, **far exceeding** every other move of God, including the great move which transpired at the **birth of the Church and beginning of the Church Age** on the Day of Pentecost. In its totality, it will also be **the last great restorational move of God** and will effect the **culmination of the Church Age**.

Now, the **GOOD NEWS** about this great move of God is that IT HAS ALREADY BEGUN! The **restoration of the PROPHET'S** ministry back into its rightful place of function within the Church is the beginning of the winds of restoration that will crescendo into the grand finale of this last great tidal wave restorational move! The **Elijah Company of Prophets** is being manifested now in order to bring forth the **purification** of the Church to make her ready for **glorification**.

1 Pet. 4:17 Simultaneously, though not coincidentally, with the restoration of the Prophets has also come **"judgment of the Household of God."** The ultimate result of this final restorational movement will be—**the PERFECTION of the Church!** However, it will begin with the **PURIFICATION** of the Church, that is, "judgment of the Household of God," which judgment is a judgment that will result not in **DAMNATION**, as will the ensuing judgment of the world, but in the **GLORIFICATION** of the Church (topic of the next lesson).

Rev. 19:7 This restorational move will be **"the Bride mak(ing) herself ready (fit, prepared)"** for presentation to the Bridegroom at the **Marriage Supper of the Lamb**. This final tidal wave of restoration shall **"clear the way" for the return of Christ** to claim His Church-Bride and the "catching up" of the Church-Bride into Heaven for the Marriage Supper of the Lamb.

Heb. 6:2 As discussed in the previous Section, this restorational move in its entirety will constitute the restoration and the actual fulfillment of the fifth foundational doctrine of the Church—**The Resurrection of the Dead**. The **GLORIFICATION AND RESURRECTION** of the Church, which shall culminate with the "catching up" of the Church-Bride **(1 Thes. 4:15-17)**, shall give way to that great and awful **"DAY OF THE LORD"**, the day of the execution of the eternal judgment of God upon the ungodly and unbelieving **(2 Thes. 2:1-12)**, which is the restoration and fulfillment of the last foundational doctrine of the Church—**ETERNAL JUDGMENT**.

2 Kgs. 2:1-15; Jn. 14:12 The work of the prophets during this move will be accomplished under the unction of the **"Elijah Anointing."** As mentioned before, the period in which the "Elijah Anointing" rests upon the Church will be followed by a period in which the **"Elisha Anointing"** falls upon the entire Body of Christ. This will be the **"double-portion anointing"** in which, as promised by Jesus, the corporate Body of Christ will not only replicate the works

A Biblical Perspective of the Prophetic Gifts and Office

of power Jesus performed, but will be empowered to perform **"even greater works"** than He did, in the same manner as Elisha was empowered to perform **"double"** the miracles Elijah did after inheriting his mentor's anointing.

Hag. 2:9 The prophecy of Haggai that "the latter glory of this house will be greater than the former" will have its ultimate fulfillment when the "Elisha Anointing" comes upon the Church. The works of supernatural power that will be manifested under the unction of that "Elisha (double-portion) Anointing" will totally eclipse the abundant displays of supernatural power enacted through the early Apostles and disciples at the beginning of the Church Age. When this powerful anointing comes upon the Church, the corporate Body of Christ, like Jesus during His earthly ministry, will have the anointing "without measure," and literally countless numbers of miracles, signs, and wonders will be wrought through the hands of ordinary believers all over the world.

STRUCTURAL REFORMATION COMING

In addition to **SPIRITUAL RESTORATION**, extensive **STRUCTURAL REFORMATION** will also take place during this coming tidal wave move of God.

Mat. 9:17 The **"OLD WINESKINS"** cannot contain the **"NEW WINE"** (New revelation and power) to be released in the coming move of God. **THE "NEW WINE" MUST BE POURED INTO "NEW WINESKINS!"** The greater revelation that God will be revealing through the Apostles and Prophets in this next move **(Eph. 3:3-5)** cannot be poured into ministry organizations in their present structural configuration. The new revelation that is coming must be poured into structurally reformed ministries. The coming move of God will bring not only the *spiritual* **RESTORATION** but also the *structural* **REFORMATION** necessary to make churches and ministries spiritually and structurally ready and prepared to receive the greater revelation and exaltation that is coming. To say it another way: in order for the Church to become "glorifiable," we must have both *spiritual* **restoration** and *structural* **reformation**.

"Reform," "restructure," "reconstruct," were the divinely-inspired "buzz words" around the turn of the decade of the 90's. Reformation and restructuring began taking place in governments and nations all over the world. Europe, fulfilling Bible prophecy, began reorganizing, restructuring, and negotiating reunification. The European union became a reality in 1992. The Berlin Wall suddenly came down overnight in 1989, and the reunification of divided Germany also is now a reality. The Soviet Union, per se, no longer exists, and has undergone massive "re-formation" and reorganization, with many of its republics seceding and others threatening same. The Iron Curtain is being dismantled bit by bit. Ironically enough, it was the then Soviet Premier, Gorbechov, who popularized the Russian term **"perestroika"** as a slogan to capsulize his program for reform in the Soviet Union. And, what does the term "perestroika" mean? Would you believe? — **"restructure!"** Gorbechov was chosen by God to be a present-day "Cyrus" of sorts, an unbelieving world leader who is a mere pawn under the hand of God, to start the machinery of world restructure for the fulfillment of the master end-time plan of God. It was necessary for restructure to take place in the European and Soviet Block nations in order to coincide with end-time Bible prophecy.

Hag. 2:7; Heb. 12:26-27 All the upheaval taking place throughout the nations of the world right now is far from being accidental or coincidental. It is all a part of God's perfectly designed master plan for the ages. God promised to shake literally **"every nation,"** which is exactly what is taking place on a global basis at this very moment. Every government in the world is being shaken to its very core, and what we are witnessing now is only the beginning—major governmental "shake-ups" will yet take place even in countries where many think it just cannot happen. God's word promises that all this will indeed take place. God's promise to shake all that can be shaken is recorded:

> "And **HIS VOICE SHOOK THE EARTH** then, but now He has promised, saying, **"YET ONCE MORE I WILL SHAKE NOT ONLY THE EARTH, BUT ALSO THE HEAVEN."** And this expression, "Yet once more," denotes the removing of those things which can be shaken, as of created things, in order that those things which cannot be shaken may **REMAIN**. Therefore, since we have **a KINGDOM which CANNOT BE SHAKEN,** let us show gratitude, by which we may offer to God an acceptable service with reverence and awe; for our God is a consuming fire."

Rev. 11:15 The conquest of Christ will climax when "the kingdoms of this world have become the **Kingdoms of our Lord and of His Christ**, and He shall reign forever." Kingdoms which have been built as possessions of men, will be toppled in the coming shaking, so that the only kingdom which will remain standing will be the **KINGDOM OF GOD.** Jesus will be the only remaining monarch when all is accomplished. Those who have been building their little kingdoms in which they have exalted themselves as some sort of an icon now had better repent quickly and humble themselves, lest in the days that are upon us they be abruptly humiliated. Despite this warning and similar warnings that will come from others, there will still be leaders of some ministries who will refuse to take heed and who will in the very near future suddenly come to the end of the rope they have been given and will hang themselves, so to speak. Many who have become arrogant in their self-made domains in which they have reigned supreme and have been deceived into thinking that their sovereignty was absolute, have unbeknownst to them been "set up" by the devil for a great fall. Those who refuse to repent will be violently and suddenly dethroned. Their destruction will come upon them as a thief in the night with none to help and without remedy!

1 Cor. 15:46 "The spiritual is not first, but the natural; then the spiritual." Events taking place in the natural realm are usually a mere preview of what is about to take place in the spiritual realm. What takes place in the nations is a reflection of what is going to take place in the Church. Such was the case with the **earthquakes** also transpiring at the turn of this decade in California which were so destructive. They were divine forewarning of the **"shaking"** that is about to hit the Church at large. As I watched with great concern the news accounts of the devastation wrought during the earthquakes in which so many buildings were razed to the ground and even ultra-modern megastructure bridges and highway overpasses collapsed in a moment of time, the Lord said to me, "What you are seeing take place in the natural is what is going to take place in the spiritual in many ministry organizations."

This shaking has already begun! It is the JUDGMENT OF THE HOUSEHOLD OF GOD (1 Pet. 4:17) which must come precedent to judgment of the world. Several years before this writing, I prophesied by the Spirit in my prophetic seminars that a major time of shaking was coming. Many people, primarily Christians, who worshipped their lifestyles of ease and comfort greatly disliked and were frightened by many of the prophesies that came forth in my seminars. Christians, a la the world, have become worshippers of "peace and safety," and it is that very idolatry that will cause many of them to be deceived in the last days apostasy by the New Age false prophets. Even as I write these words, much shaking is taking place in many ministry organizations just as the prophecies said. Many prominent ministries are undergoing major structural changes now. Some simply outlived their usefulness and have been (or soon will be) disassembled and disbanded altogether under divine directive from the Lord. Others are now realizing that God did not truly inspire and has refused divine sponsorship of their expansion programs, and thus have had to pare back their operations. Still others have been unwillingly forced to restructure their ministries.

Acts 27 The story of the Apostle Paul's voyage en route to Rome has remarkable correlations to what will take place in this movement, in terms of ministries who attempt to continue to "do their own thing" contrary to the restorational and reformational winds of the Spirit which are now blowing in the Church. Those ministries which refuse to listen to the admonitions of the Apostles and Prophets God is raising up to speak forth His divine plan for the Church, and who refuse to alter their course to flow with the spiritual winds that God is now causing to blow, are going to find themselves shipwrecked and their ship destroyed.

Bound to the Centurion accompanying him, Paul was traveling to Rome to appeal his case before Caesar. As the ship they were aboard on the first leg of their journey sailed on the course set by the captain of ship, soon "the winds were contrary" (v. 4). Similarly, the leadership of many ministries today have set their own self-determined course toward what is often a self-aggrandizing destination. Many of those ministries, however, will soon be discovering that the winds of spiritual restoration and structural reformation God is now causing to blow are blowing unflaggingly "contrary" against them, inhibiting their progress.

Even after changing ships to board an Alexandrian ship sailing for Italy, the sojourners made very little headway against the contrary winds: "And when we had sailed slowly for a good many days and with difficulty had arrived off Cnidus, since **the wind did not permit us to go farther**...." In an analogous manner, the winds of restoration and reformation will continue to blow contrary against many God-ordained ministries, not permitting them to go any farther, until they amend their course to sail toward a God-appointed destination.

> "And when considerable time had passed and the voyage was now dangerous...Paul began to admonish them, and said to them, '**Men, I perceive that the voyage will certainly be attended with damage and great loss, not only of the cargo and the ship, but also of our lives.**'"

So also, warnings of impending, but avoidable, devastation are even now being trumpeted forth by some prophets hearing the leadings of the Spirit unto the "captains" of many ministries and their passengers. They perceive damage and great loss to the ship as well as spiritual devastation unto the passengers of ships if the call to course-change is not heeded. If these ministries are more persuaded by the mind-set of tradition than by the warnings of the Spirit, as those traveling with Paul were more persuaded by the "expertise" of the captain of the ship than they were by the Spirit-inspired warning given by Paul, many of them will suffer similar results as Paul's shipmates—destruction of their ships, i.e., their ministries **(Ac. 27:11ff)**.

The result of all that is coming will be that God will finally have His way in the true Church as Jesus reclaims His rightful place as the true functional Head of the Church which He purchased with His own blood. He emphatically proclaimed, "**I will build MY Church.**"

For years now, however, men have been building **THEIR** private kingdoms, financed with God's money, which they have elicited from God's people based on their claims that all their ambitions were "of the Lord." But, now the Lord has begun to withdraw divine funding and sponsorship of many of those private kingdoms. Every existing God-led and God-ordained ministry is going to go through refinement fires unto purification, compelling them to make the changes necessary to be "established in present truth" **(2 Pet. 1:12)** and the structural reform necessary to make the "wineskin" what it needs to be in order to truly be "about the Father's business" until Jesus returns. (*More on this refinement and purification in the next chapter.*)

Now it is absolutely essential to understand that all of these projections regarding coming restoration and restructuring refer **only** to bona fide candelstick, present-truth church-cells of **Jesus' "CHURCH"** -- the one that He Himself is building. That is to say, local churches that are a "candlestick church" because they were originally **born** of the Spirit (nature), corporately they are earnestly endeavoring to **walk** by the Spirit (fruit), and they bear the **signs** of the Spirit (manifestation gifts of the Spirit); thus, they bear the **seal** (witness) of the Spirit. Nevertheless, though their entire existence and purpose is centered in the Spirit of God, these churches by no means exalt the Spirit as sovereign or Lord, for they are well aware that the role of the third Person of the Godhead is to give witness of and exalt Jesus Christ as the sovereign Lord and absolute Head of the Church. Rather, what these churches exalt, extol, and call all men to, is not the **Spirit** of God, but the **Son** of God — the **WORD** of God, "the Word made flesh...(who) dwelt among us." These churches exalt the **DOCTRINE** (i.e., the teaching) of **God's WORD**, rather than the **deeds** of God's Spirit, though they wholeheartdly believe in, pray for, and are exceedingly thankful for the deeds or acts of the Holy Spirit in their midst. All this is what makes them "Present-Truth" churches.

It is these present-truth, candlestick churches that will be a part of the massive renovation, or structural reformation, of the Church that is coming. The thousands of so-called "churches," whole denominations, and groups of churches that elect to continue operating outside of these parameters will not have a part in this restoration and reformation, but rather will go right on reveling in their subtle *delusions* and *deceptions* (partial truth) and, unfortunately, the resultant *destructions* (Hos. 4:6) which the enemy is given leave to wreak in the lives of their members "because they did not receive the love of the truth" (2 Thes. 2:9-12), as well.

A Biblical Perspective of the Prophetic Gifts and Office

LESSON 15
PURIFICATION AND GLORIFICATION

THE GLORIFICATION OF THE CHURCH

God is about to dramatically increase the anointing upon the entire Body of Christ. The "spirit of wisdom and revelation" (Eph. 1:17) is being increased upon the Church to bring forth greater revelation and understanding of spiritual Truth. In short, the Lord is about to **GLORIFY** the Bride, the Lamb's wife.

GLORIFICATION of the Church: Jn. 17:22; Is. 42:1,8/48:1-11; Rom. 8:18, 29-30; 2 Cor. 3:18, 4:17; 1 Pet. 5:10; 2 Thes. 2:14; 2 Tim. 2:10; 1 Sam. 2:8 (KJV); Plp. 2:5-11; Jas 4:10.

The above passages are just a few of those in Scripture which establish as a spiritual fact the matter of the exaltation and glorification of the Church. In order for the Church, both collectively and individually, to be ready and prepared for **GLORIFICATION**, it must first go through **PURIFICATION**.

Mat. 9:17 The "OLD WINESKINS" cannot contain the "NEW WINE" (New revelation and power) to be released in the coming move of God. **THE "NEW WINE" MUST BE POURED INTO "NEW WINESKINS"!**

Thus, the coming move of God will bring *spiritual* **RESTORATION** to the Church as well as *structural* **REFORMATION** to churches and ministries. We must have both before the Lord can effect the glorification of the Church as His Eternal Bride!

THE PURIFICATION OF THE CHURCH

Eph. 5:27 THE CHURCH WITHOUT SPOT OR WRINKLE

A pure and chaste Church is the Bride Jesus is coming back to claim for Himself, a Church **"without SPOT or WRINKLE or any such thing."**

"Spots" The term "spots" or "blemishes" could very well refer to the doctrinal flaws which still exist in the Church. The **spiritual restoration** that is coming by way of an unveiling of greater revelation through the ministry of the Apostles and Prophets is what will remove those spots and blemishes. Until these flaws are removed the Church will remain to be imperfect and immature, and Christ is not coming back for a "pimply-faced," undeveloped, immature, adolescent girl to claim as His Bride. Rather, He will remain in Heaven until the Bride has become fully mature **(Ac. 3:21; Eph. 4:13)**. Blemishes in an animal breed indicates that breed has some impurities in its genetic lineage. Jesus was the "**SPOTLESS** Lamb of God." He was the "pure breed" of the Divine genetic Family. The Lord will return when His Church-Bride has become fully "established in present Truth." In other words, at the return of Christ, the true Church of Jesus will be doctrinally pure and spiritually perfected, so as to be the very embodiment of the pure revelation of the very **"Mind of Christ"** (1 Cor. 2:16). The Church will also be a "pure breed" without "spots" or "blemishes." The complete sanctification spoken of in **First**

A Biblical Perspective of the Prophetic Gifts and Office

Thessalonians 5:23 must have corporate application as well as individual. Though our "spirit" is pure and holy, we are in the process of being made holy in our "soul" realm, which is headquartered in the mind, so that the process of sanctification we are undergoing now is in the realm of what we "think."

"Wrinkles" The term "wrinkles" could be a reference to the outward antiquated "structural" condition of the "wine **skins**." Wrinkles are a condition of the skin associated with **aging**. Just as Christ is not coming back to claim an immature little girl as His Bride, neither is He returning for a crusty, haggard, irascible, contentious, set-in-her-ways, old shrew. Yet, that is precisely what the people of many churches are like—they are so set in their ways like cement in a sidewalk and they're not about to do any changing. The mere mention of the word "change" causes tangible waves of terror to ripple through most congregations. But, any church that is not undergoing constant evolutionary change is a church that is dying, though it thinks it lives. Every church would do well to remember that **the last words of a dying church are: "We've never done it this way before."**

Lk. 5:39 The vast majority of Christians are like those Jesus described who do not want the new wine, but say, "The old wine is good enough." The theme song of most churches should be "I Will Not Be Moved." "Give me that old-time religion," many proudly sing. For some inexplicable reason, much of mankind is inclined toward the idiotic idea that maintaining the status quo and avoiding change is somehow the very epitome of virtue. In many ways, many people's definition of success is: avoidance of change. We consider maintaining the status quo to be so noble that we all but canonize the person who was so "virtuous" that all his life he lived in the same house, worked for the same company, drove the same car, and drank the same brand of coffee made in the same coffee pot out of the same cup. Today, many seem to be smitten with a kind of "nostalgimania" in which they are nearly obsessed with things from past eras, to the point that they'll pay exorbitant prices for almost anything from bygone eras which has been dignified with the appellation— "antique."

Somehow, despite our superior intellectual sophistication, it escapes the notice of most that, like the statues we erect to immortalize the mortal, the only things that do not change are those which have ceased to live or which never had life in the first place. Every living creature in God's vast cosmos undergoes constant change. Continuous metamorphosis is that estate which we call "life."

The truth of the matter is that resistance to change is not virtuous, nor is it godly, and God is not at all pleased with our stubbornness and stiffnecked rebellion to His calls for change. Resistance to change is resistance to God, for God, though He Himself never changes **(Mal. 3:6)** because perfection cannot be improved upon, is a God of change who is forever sponsoring and in many cases generating change. God is a God of **new things**, and says,

> "Behold, the former things have come to pass, now I declare **NEW THINGS**; before they spring forth I proclaim them to you." **(Is. 42:9)**
> "Do not call to mind the former things, or ponder things of the past. Behold, I will do something **NEW**, now it will spring forth; will you not be aware of it?" **(Is. 43:18,19)**

Rom. 8:29 This verse has not only individual but also corporate application. God is orchestrating change in the Body of Christ, change that is designed to further conform us into the image of Christ. God does nothing that is superfluous or unnecessary. God orchestrates change because it is necessary, and thus for obedient believers, it is **never optional**, but is **always obligatory**. **The Church needs change to remove the wrinkles of age.** To use a modern metaphor, the Church is due for a spiritual **"face-lift"** of sorts to remove those wrinkles.

Rev. 19:7,8 The bride makes *herself* ready

Adorns herself with **FINE LINEN — RIGHTEOUS ACTS**

Rev. 21:1,2 A bride adorned (with righteousness, purity) — the church

1 Pet. 4:17 Judgment must begin with the household of God

Heb. 10:26-31 God will judge his people!!!

Heb. 12:18-29 Our God is a consuming fire!!! God promises to SHAKE the Church (Mount Zion)

FIRE OF PURIFICATION AND REFINEMENT!

Lam. 4:11-13 FIRE IN ZION (the Church)!!!

Luke 12:49 Jesus came to CAST FIRE on the Earth

Mat. 3:11,12 Jesus baptizes with Holy Spirit AND FIRE

Rev. 1:12-15 An OMNIPOTENT Jesus — In the midst of the churches

EYES — Fire = **REFINER**
FEET — Burnished Brass = **JUDGE**

Is. 33:10-13 Breath of GOD (HOLY SPIRIT) will consume like a FIRE!!! Sinners in Zion are terrified!!!

Zech. 13:8,9 One-third remnant (true believers) — refined by fire

Is. 48:1-10 House of Jacob (loins of Judah) — refined in furnace of affliction

Ps. 105:16-19 REFINING OF JOSEPH (= CHURCH)

REFINEMENT precedes **Ruling & Reigning**

Corporate Church must be **refined** by fire to prepared and ready to **rule & reign** with Christ

Mal. 3:1-5 JESUS COMES TO HIS TEMPLE (THE CHURCH)

He is like a **REFINERS FIRE** and a **FULLER'S SOAP**

He sits as a **SMELTER & PURIFIER** of silver.

He comes to **PURIFY the sons of Levi (Ministers)** and refine them like gold and silver. Result: the ministers present **OFFERINGS IN RIGHTEOUSNESS** (righteous, obedient saints) to the Lord.

He will draw near in **JUDGMENT**, against —

> sorcerers (Jezebels, and those who dominate)
> adulterers (sexual and spiritual)
> those who swear falsely (false teachers and leaders)
> those who oppress wage earners in their wages
> those who oppress widows and orphans
> those who turn aside sojourners or travelers
> those who do not fear God

1 Cor. 3:11-15 EVERY BELIEVER will be REFINED BY FIRE

Each individual believer must be refined in order to be able to rule & reign with Christ.

MINISTRIES (work of ministers) will be **PURGED BY FIRE**. Every ministry will go through refinement fires to purify them in order that the true God-appointed ministries of God will be even more productive and useful.

1 Pet. 4:12 PURPOSE of Fire—**TESTING, PURIFYING, REFINING.**

1 Pet. 1:3-7 RESULT of Fire—**TRUE, PURIFIED FAITH.**

Jas. 1:12 REWARD of **ENDURING** Purification Fire—**CROWN OF ETERNAL LIFE**

LESSON 16
THE ELIJAH COMPANY OF PROPHETS IN THE COMING RESTORATION AND PURIFICATION

THE ELIJAH COMPANY OF PROPHETS USHER IN THE TIDAL WAVE

The **PROPHETS** will usher in this next great move of God! The **PROPHETS** prepare the way and the Church-Bride for the **SECOND COMING** of Christ as John the Baptist prepared the way for the **FIRST COMING** of Christ! As mentioned before, it is not mere coincidence that this move is happening simultaneously with the restoration of the Apostles and Prophets back into their rightful place in the Church. The **APOSTLES AND PROPHETS** will be the primary catalysts for change in this next great move of God!

Rev. 19:7, 8 The Bride makes HERSELF ready (prepared). As we shall see, it is the role of the prophets and the apostles to prepare and make the Church-Bride ready for the return of Christ to claim His Church-Bride for Eternal marriage. Since Apostles and prophets are themselves also members of the Body of Christ, their restorational work on behalf of God, is the Bride making **HERSELF** ready.

THE ELIJAH COMPANY OF PROPHETS—raised up to RESTORE AND PREPARE

Ac. 3:21 RESTORATION is the ministry of Prophets.

Is. 42:18-22 "NONE SAYETH, 'RESTORE'" (KJV); **Joel 2:23-26** "I WILL RESTORE"

None sayeth "**restore**," so the Lord Himself pledges to get involved in the matter of restoration. Yet, we must be always mindful of the fact that God does nothing on Earth apart from His Body. **We**, believers, are His Body, His hands, His feet, His mouth. When God says, "*I will*," He means **He** will, but *through some member(s) of His Body.* God is always looking for those who will obey Him to perform His purposes through them. In this next move, God will perform His purposes through prophets and apostles who after having "been through the grinding mill" of God's "breaking and making" program are now willing to obey God despite the resistance they encounter and regardless of the degree of difficulty of the assignment.

Eph. 4:7-13 APOSTLES AND PROPHETS are part of the Fivefold ministries Jesus has given to the Church to equip and develop the Body, both individually and collectively.

Eph. 2:20 APOSTLES AND PROPHETS are **THE FOUNDATIONAL MINISTRIES** of the Church.

1 Cor. 12:28 GOD has **permanently SET** the foundational ministries of Apostles and Prophets within the Church.

Mal. 4:5,6 God will send Elijah the Prophet immediately before the "day of (the judgment) God"—to **RESTORE**.

Lk. 1:11-17 The Elijah anointing (ministry) is a **PROPHET'S** ministry of **POWER**. Elijah will come to **RESTORE** (turn back) — to **make ready a people prepared** for the Lord. John The Baptist was an **Elijah TO ISRAEL**.

Mat. 11:7-14 John the Baptist was the Elijah Prophet — **to Israel** — who came to **PREPARE THE WAY** for the **first coming of Christ**.

Rev. 11:3-12 The **TWO WITNESSES** are **APOSTLES (MOSES) AND PROPHETS (ELIJAH)**.

> **Mat. 16:27-17:13** Mt. of Transfiguration event — **THE SON OF MAN COMING IN HIS KINGDOM**.
>
> **Rev. 11:1-10, 15** **MOSES** (Law) and **ELIJAH** (Power) appeared with Jesus — **THE TWO WITNESSES** — whose end-time ministry will usher in the Kingdom of God.
>
> **Mat. 11:13** "For all the **prophets** and the **Law** prophesied (of the coming of the Messiah and His Kingdom) **until John**" — "the **Word** of His **Power**" (Heb. 1:3).
>
> **(v. 11)** "Elijah is (shall, is going to be) coming [future tense] and will **RESTORE ALL THINGS** ('about which the prophets spoke from ancient times' [Ac. 3:21])."

MAL. 4:5 PROPHETS — THE ELIJAHS TO COME

God promised to **send ELIJAH THE PROPHET OF POWER immediately** "BEFORE the great and terrible day of the Lord" (that is, the day of God's judgment of the world). The ministry of this Elijah will be **RESTORATION**.

2 Kgs. 2:11 The actual man Elijah was **taken up into Heaven** by a whirlwind on chariots of fire. And, God does not work by reincarnation. So, what does this mean?

Lk. 1:17 Gabriel explained by saying Elijah would return in the symbolic sense of a resurgence of Elijah's ministry — **the prophets ministry of POWER and the SPIRIT**. The term **"spirit"** used here refers to the **"anointing"**, or the **"ministry gifting"** of the Prophet.

> **2 Cor. 3:6 (KJV)** "ministers...of the **Spirit**...." The Apostle Paul here points out a subtle but profoundly important distinction between two different types of ministers. One type of minister is the minister of the **"gramma"** [Greek], which refers to the "written" Word, or we could say the "Logos" of the Word. This type of minister "rightly divides" the Word; he is an accurate "technician" of the written Word; what he preaches is correct; yet it is without inspiration (God-breathed) of the Spirit, and therefore dry and lifeless, and does not minister "Life" unto the hearers. In order to effectively impart spiritual revelation unto others one must not only be an accurate divider of the **Truth**, but he must also minister through the inspiration of the **Spirit (Jn. 4:23,24)**. The other type of minister Paul identifies is a "minister of the Spirit," which is a minister who is truly anointed by the Spirit, and who ministers not only under the inspiration of the Spirit, but he actually imparts the "Spirit" unto the receivers, He does not merely make a well-organized presentation of truthful precepts and principles, but actually imparts the Spirit, His ministry is not predicated on the sophistication of his presentation, his oratorical skills and elocution, or even the correctness of his message, but rather on the supernatural unction of the

Spirit, that is, **"the anointing."** The only true ministry is that which takes place in the Spirit realm, not in the mental realm; from Spirit to spirit, not from mind to mind.

1 Kgs. 17 - 2 Kgs. 2:11 In these chapters we are presented the chronicles of Elijah's ministry, which can be appropriately characterized as a "ministry of **POWER**." Thus, Elijah was a **"Prophet of Power."**

LK. 1:11-17 JOHN THE BAPTIST—THE FIRST ELIJAH TO COME

John The Baptist was the **FIRST Elijah to come**, who came **to prepare the way for the FIRST COMING OF CHRIST.**

(v. 16) John The Baptist was sent to the **SONS OF ISRAEL**. He came in the spirit and power of Elijah to turn the hearts of the **SONS OF ISRAEL** back to the Lord their God, that is to say, to prepare the **JEWS** for their visitation by the Lord—the **FIRST COMING of Christ.**

Is. 40:3 God foretold that He would send a **special messenger** to **prepare the way for the first coming of the Lord**—

Mat. 3:1-3 John The Baptist was the first fulfillment of this—he prepared the way for the **FIRST COMING of Christ**.

Mat. 11:7-14 Jesus said John the Baptist was a **PROPHET** and **"more than a prophet"**—he was the **"Elijah"** who was to come prior to the first coming of Christ and the **special messenger** of whom Isaiah prophesied.

Mat. 17:11-13 "Elijah **IS** coming and **will restore ALL THINGS**; but I say to you that Elijah **already came**...." In this passage **Jesus** indicated **ANOTHER ELIJAH** other than John The Baptist is yet to come. John The Baptist was the first fulfillment of the Elijah to come, who came to prepare the way for the Messiah's **FIRST** coming, but could not possibly have been the only Elijah to come because Jesus said the Elijah who would come would **"restore ALL THINGS"**, yet, John The Baptist did not "restore all things." In fact, because of the rejection of Jesus by the Jews, he restored **nothing** except for being instrumental in causing some in the House of Israel to believe in the coming Messiah. Thus, of necessity it seems, there shall be yet **"another Elijah"** who will come and who *WILL* **"restore all things."** As mentioned, John The Baptist was the "Elijah" sent to the **Jewish nation**. The Elijah who will "restore all things" of necessity speaks of "another Elijah" other than John the Baptist who would be sent not to the Jewish nation but to **the Church** in order to **"restore all things** about which God spoke through the mouth of His holy prophets from ancient times" **(Ac. 3:21)**

Lk. 1:17 This verse gives us yet another indication that another "Elijah" other than John The Baptist would come. Gabriel indicated that the ministry of Elijah would be **"to make ready A PEOPLE prepared for the Lord."** The Apostle Peter, himself a Jew, declared that it was not Israel but the **CHURCH** who was now the **"PEOPLE of God"** which Elijah will make ready and prepared for the coming of the Lord **(1 Pet. 2:10)**. (In Christ Jesus there is neither male nor female, **Jew** nor Greek, but only true **"BELIEVERS."** The Church is now the only **"Chosen Race"** and the only **"Holy Nation"** [**1 Pet. 2:9**].) Thus, John The Baptist could not have possibly been the fulfillment of this prophecy in its entirety because his ministry was not to the Church but to the nation of **ISRAEL**, which fact was further accentuated by his death *prior* to the crucifixion of Christ and the birth of the Church.

A Biblical Perspective of the Prophetic Gifts and Office

Conclusion: The **ELIJAH COMPANY OF PROPHETS** God is now raising up to usher in the culminating restorational movement **are the ULTIMATE FULFILLMENT OF THE PREDICTED COMING "ELIJAH."** John the Baptist was the singular fulfillment of the coming of the first "Elijah" who was prophesied to come, but the second "Elijah" to come will not be a singular prophet, but rather a **"COMPANY OF PROPHETS."**

THE ROLE OF THE ELIJAH COMPANY OF PROPHETS IN THE COMING MOVEMENT

Is. 40:3 THE ELIJAH COMPANY OF PROPHETS will **PREPARE** the way for the **SECOND COMING** of Christ.

Lk. 1:17; Rev. 19:7,8; Rev. 21:2; Eph. 4:11-13; Eph. 5:25-27 THE ELIJAH COMPANY OF PROPHETS will **MAKE READY** a people (The Church) **PREPARED** for the Lord.

Rev. 10:7; 11:15 The ministry of the **COMPANY OF PROPHETS** will bring the **culmination of the Church Age**.

Ac. 3:21 When the **prophets** have finished their ministry of preparing the Church-Bride and making her ready for the Bride-groom, **Christ will be released** to return to claim the Church as His Eternal Bride.

Ezk. 37:1-14 THE PROPHETS WILL EQUIP THE ARMY OF THE LORD. As discussed previously, it is the **prophesying of the prophets** that will transform the Church from a "valley of dry bones" into a unified, matured, **exceedingly great ARMY of the Lord.** The Church of Jesus Christ is foreordained and predestined to become—**"an exceedingly great ARMY of the Lord."**

Joel 2:1-11 Description of the **ARMY OF THE LORD.** Verses seven and eight delineate two important qualities of the end-time army of the Lord: they **ALL march in line** and **do not break ranks**. This speaks of the **Divine Order** that will be the hallmark of the Lord's Army, the Church. Members of the Lord's Army shall willingly submit themselves to God's appointed and delegated authority, not breaking ranks or getting out of line to manifest themselves in rebellious selfish ambition, self-exaltation, or deeds of self-aggrandizement.

> **Heb. 13:17** "Obey your leaders; and submit to them; for they keep watch over your souls.
>
> **1 Pet. 5:5,6** "...be subject (**submit**, KJV) **to your elders**...humble yourselves under the mighty **hand of God**" (one application of the term "the hand of God" is the Fivefold ministry officers of God's Army.)

However, it is vital in discussing this matter of the saints' subordination in this last day Army of God that we understand clearly that this is a **WILLING** subjection by the saints unto the leadership of the true Davidic shepherds God will have raised up in the last day, not one of coercion and domination by heavy-handed, despotic, so-called "leaders" over the people of God. When this last day Army of the Lord is formulated, the shepherds who have been dominating the sheep and who like Saul engaged in forms of demonic control, i.e., witchcraft, over the sheep, will have all been removed from their self-imposed monarchial thrones. They will have ceased from being shepherds, and from dominating the sheep with "force (coercion) and severity," and the Lord will have caused the sheep to revolt from following after those shepherds, will scatter the flock of those shepherds, and will lead His true sheep to true shepherds after the heart of God, like unto David, who will cause them to rest in green pastures, will lead them beside peaceful waters of life, will restore their souls, and will guide them in the paths of true righteousness (Jer. 23:4; Ezk. 34; Ps. 23).

No one is authorized by the Word of God to control and dominate, or subjugate another person. The words translated as "submit" and "obey" in the above passages and in some others in Scripture do not connote a "ruling over" others; rather, they simply mean to be yielding, pliable, teachable, persuadable, to put confidence in, to listen to, to rely upon, those whom God has set into the Body of Christ to provide the pilotage of the ship, i.e., Fivefold ministers.

(For more on this topic, readers are urged to read the book, *Charismatic Captivation* and the booklet, *Charismatic Control*, both of which were also written by the author of this manual.)

LESSON 17
RESTORATION, REFORMATION, REVOLUTION, AND RESISTERS

REJECTION BY SOME THEOLOGIANS OF THE PREMISE OF RESTORATION OF THE PROPHETIC MINISTRY.

John the Baptist was the **GREATEST SIGN** ever given signifying the **first coming** of the Messiah to the people of that day. His coming to prepare the way for the coming of the Messiah was prophesied by several of the prophets.

Mat. 17:12 But, the spiritually blind religious **scribes, Pharisees, and Sadducees,** the theologians of the time, **did not recognize** the significance of John's ministry. So, they rejected John and his ministry, as well as the Messiah of whom he came to bear witness, and eventually demanded His crucifixion.

So also, most theologians and the majority of denominational ministers of this day will **fail to recognize THE GREATEST SIGN of this age** signifying the imminent **second coming** of Christ—**THE ELIJAH COMPANY OF PROPHETS** being raised up by the Lord to prepare the way for the return of Christ, who will return to **take personal and literal dominion over the "kingdoms of this world"** (Rev. 10:7; 11:15).

Rev. 11:15 Christ's first coming was for to be **rejected** and to **redeem** the many. His second coming will be to **REIGN**—over all the kingdoms of this world.

Many theologians look to events occurring in Israel as an indicator of the nearness of the return of Christ. Though events in Israel are a spiritual barometer, as the moon is a reflection of the sun, so also Israel is now merely a reflection of what is happening in the Church.

The **CHURCH**—Spiritual Israel—is who Jesus is coming back to claim as His Bride, not the nation of Israel. Peter, a Jew, declared that it is not Israel that is now "the people of God, but rather—the Church of the redeemed, blood-washed, Born Again, Spirit-filled believers: **"for you once were not a people, but now you are THE PEOPLE OF GOD"** (1 Pet. 2:10).

Rom. 2:28,29 "He is not a Jew who is one outwardly...but he is a Jew who is one inwardly." **In Christ Jesus** there is neither male nor female, **Jew nor Greek**, only true **"BELIEVERS."** Believers are now the **only "CHOSEN RACE"** and the **only "HOLY NATION"** (1 Pet. 2:9).

Those looking to the nation of Israel as the sign of the nearness of the second coming of Christ are going to totally miss **THE GREATEST SIGN in 2,000 years** of the imminence of the return of Christ—**the restoration of the PROPHETS MINISTRY! THE ULTIMATE PURPOSE OF THE UNIVERSE IS THE *CHURCH*!** The nation of Israel is not the ultimate objective of the Divine Plan of God for the Universe, but rather it is a small group of redeemed, blood-washed, Holy Ghost sanctified people comprising the **CHURCH, THE BRIDE OF CHRIST, THE LAMB'S WIFE (REV. 21:9)**. This is further supported by the fact that all the ages will culminate in one great event—**THE MARRIAGE SUPPER OF THE LAMB** in which Christ will be eternally wed to His Church-Bride!

A Biblical Perspective of the Prophetic Gifts and Office

ACTS 7:51 - 8:1 RESISTERS OF THE HOLY SPIRIT — HATERS OF GOD AND HIS MESSAGE, MURDERERS OF HIS MESSENGERS

The Jewish religious leaders resisted the valid move of God from the Old Covenant into the New Covenant, even though it was a "better covenant, based on better promises."

This move was of God, not men. It was not of human invention or initiative, but God's. The Pharisees and Sadduccees could not perceive that. Though the **message** was from God, they hated it. So, they persecuted and even murdered the **messengers** who proclaimed the message. Stephen was only one whom they murdered.

Jesus came proclaiming a **NEW REVELATION**—the revelation of the **NEW COVENANT**. Jesus had declared, "Believe in God, believe also in **ME**." Rightstanding with God would now be reckoned only on the basis of faith in Jesus Christ, who Himself was the fulfillment of all the Old Testament types and shadows. Rightstanding with God could no longer be reckoned on the basis of the observance of the Old Testament Laws and ordinances—the Old Covenant was now **OBSOLETE**. A **NEW ERA** had dawned, and a **NEW COVENANT** put into effect. The Old could not be maintained or reclaimed, but it had now been made forever **OBSOLETE**.

"Behold, I will do a **NEW THING**"—their Old Testament prophets declared. Now God had indeed instituted a **"NEW THING,"** but these die-hard **"defenders of the faith,"** refused to accept it. They refused the **NEW WINE** and said, **"the OLD WINE is good enough,"** as Jesus said they would. They simply could not make the adjustment to flow with the new thing God was doing. Change was an unwelcomed threat to their belief system, because their faith was not in God but in their own religion. Elimination of all potential threats to their belief system was essential. Thus, eradication of the those proclaiming this **NEW "WAY"** was also necessary. So, they killed Stephen as their forefathers had killed the prophets before him.

Ac. 7:51 These men were **RESISTING THE HOLY SPIRIT**, not men. They were resisting the work of the Holy Spirit because they were pride-filled **"STIFF-NECKED"** rebels against God, and because they were **"UNCIRCUMCISED of HEART and EARS,"** though they claimed to be so religious and devout.

The **"NEW WINE"** of the New Testament revelation could not be poured into **"OLD WINESKINS."** The Old Wineskins rejected the New Wine.

REVELATION PRODUCES REVOLUTION!

In bringing forth this **NEW REVELATION**, Jesus had Himself started a **REVOLUTION**. His faithful followers in order to remain so, found it necessary to be passive participants in a **REVOLT** against the established church. Throughout the ages of Church history, this scenario has been repeated time and time again, during Divinely appointed **"TIMES OF RESTORATION"** (Ac. 3:17-21) of revealed Truth.

When Jesus came, He came as the fulfillment and embodiment of Divine Truth. He Himself was the manifestation of the Word and the Life of God—the **"WORD OF LIFE"** as the Apostle John stated **(1 Jn. 1)**. He manifested all of both the **FRUITS** of the Spirit (The Life of God) and the **GIFTS** of the Spirit. When He had completed His mission on Earth, He had transferred unto all who would believe in Him afterwards, both the **FRUITS** of His Life and the **GIFTS** of the Spirit.

Eph. 4:7-11 In addition to those, He also delegated to certain believers His own personal set of **GIFTINGS** which He Himself possessed and through which He personally ministered — **THE Fivefold MINISTRY GIFTS**. When He departed planet Earth, all of these giftings and fruit were existent and operable, and soon were functioning through His followers.

Yet, as discussed earlier, less than **300 YEARS** after the birth of the Church on the Day of Pentecost, the deterioration of the Church during what has become known as the Dark Ages began. The deterioration rendered during this dark time was all but complete. All that Jesus had left behind was in the process of being abrogated and abandoned. His teachings (doctrine) were being replaced by humanistic vain philosophies of men, religious reasoning was being substituted for the gifts of the Spirit, and the Ministry Gifts were supplanted by an authoritarian religious hierarchy.

Spiritual darkness prevailed over the Church for some **1,200 years** until **October 31, 1517**, when Martin Luther nailed his **95 Thesis** to the door of the Cathedral in Wittenburg, Germany. This solitary act of protest against the Church's unScriptural practices and tenets by this previously obscure former law-student and singer turned university professor single-handedly sparked a spiritual **REVOLUTION** which came to be known as the **Protestant Reformation.**

Once again, **REVELATION** produced **REVOLUTION**, for it was the "spirit of **revelation**" that had fallen upon Luther during his research as a biblical studies professor, revealing to his heart the spiritual import of **Romans 1:17: "The just shall live by faith."** Luther described how it all began this way:

> "I greatly longed to understand Paul's Epistle to the Romans, and nothing stood in the way but that one expression, 'the righteousness of God,' because I took it to mean that righteousness whereby God is righteous and deals righteously in punishing the unrighteous. Night and day I pondered until...I grasped the truth that the righteousness of God is that righteousness whereby, through grace and sheer mercy, he justifies us by faith. **Thereupon I felt myself to be REBORN and to have gone through opened doors into paradise.** The whole Scripture took on a new meaning, and whereas before 'the righteousness of God' had filled me with hate, now it became to me inexpressibly sweet in greater love. **This passage of Paul became to me a gateway to heaven."** (Dr. Tim Dowley, *Eerdman's Handbooks to The History of Christianity*, Grand Rapids, Wm. B. Eerdman's Publishing Co., 1977. "Reform," by James Atkinson, p. 366.) [Emphases added by the author]

It was the **revelation** by the Spirit of God of this one passage of Scripture that resulted in Luther experiencing what we now refer to as being "Born Again." In effect then, it was **revelation** that produced the **"REVOLUTION"** of the Protestant Reformation, which was the inception of the divinely appointed **"TIMES OF RESTORATION"** about which the Apostle Peter prophesied nearly 1500 years before.

That process of restoration and reform that Martin Luther sparked the better part of 500 years ago is still on-going today and will continue until **"ALL THINGS** about which the prophets spoke from ancient times" are restored. It was these God-initiated **"TIMES OF RESTORATION"** that effected the PROTESTANT REFORMATION, HOLINESS MOVE-

A Biblical Perspective of the Prophetic Gifts and Office

MENT, PENTECOSTAL MOVEMENT, HEALING MOVEMENT, CHARISMATIC MOVEMENT, the present **PROPHETIC MOVEMENT** and will also effect the coming **GOVERNMENTAL MOVEMENT** which will close out this century.

Rev. 19:10 "THE SPIRIT OF PROPHECY IS THE TESTIMONY OF JESUS"

This present wave of restoration is bringing a restoration and emphasis of the Prophetic Realm. A divine decree has been issued by God in the Spirit realm, calling for the restoration of the prophetic gifts and offices. This movement is not of human invention or initiative but divine. Because it is not of men, its implementation cannot be stopped by men. Those who insist on resisting and fighting against it, will be fighting against and resisting God Himself, Jesus Christ Himself, and the work of the Holy Spirit within the Church.

RESTORATION NECESSITATES REFORM!!

SPIRITUAL **RESTORATION** of necessity engenders the need for *STRUCTURAL* **REFORMATION.** When God initiates restoration of revealed Truth, reform is inevitable and necessary. The **"NEW WINE"** of **RESTORED TRUTH** must be placed into **"NEW WINESKINS."**

REFORMATION SEEMS TO ALWAYS NECESSITATE REVOLUTION!

Because they hated the **MESSAGE** they were proclaiming, the Pharisees and Sadducees **MURDERED** the **MESSENGERS**. Just as the Pharisees and Sadducees **RESISTED** the move of God to institute the New Covenant of Jesus, historically, every new restorational move has uncovered its own generation of stiffnecked, uncircumcised, **RESISTERS OF THE HOLY SPIRIT!**

THIS PRESENT NEW MOVE OF THE SPIRIT WILL BE NO EXCEPTION! It will also uncover a whole new breed of religious "haters of God" — stiffnecked, rebellious religious people who will stubbornly resist the Holy Spirit and his working to restore the prophetic gifts and offices to the Church. By their resistance of the Holy Spirit's work and their rejection of revealed and restored truth, many purporting believers will reveal themselves to be **"ENEMIES OF THE CROSS OF CHRIST"** (Plp. 3:18).

ACTS 8:1 "A GREAT PERSECUTION AROSE"

Then as now, in implementing Divine Truth, **JESUS HAD STARTED A REVOLUTION**. His followers had found it necessary to become participants in a **REVOLT** against the established religious system. When Truth is restored, reform must ensue. **REFORM** unfortunately often produces upheaval and **PERSECUTION**.

1 Tim. 3:12 "ALL WHO DESIRE TO LIVE GODLY IN CHRIST JESUS *WILL BE* PERSECUTED."

Just as the early disciples' faithfulness was tested in the fiery "furnace of affliction" of persecution, so also believers of this era will be given the opportunity to validate their faithfulness to God by having to endure persecution and mistreatment by misinformed, misguided, and some even malevolent religious persecutors.

"ENEMIES OF THE CROSS" EXIST YET TODAY!

Plp. 3:2 "Beware of the **DOGS** (unbelievers), beware of the **EVIL WORKERS,** beware of the **FALSE CIRCUMCISION;** for we are the true circumcision, who worship in the **SPIRIT** of God and glory in **CHRIST JESUS,** and put no confidence in the flesh."

"DOGS" Refers to unbelievers. We are believers only to the extent of our acceptance of the Truth, and unbelievers to the extent of our rejection of certain portions of the Truth.

"EVIL WORKERS" can be attributed to people who, while purporting to be laboring on behalf of Christ, malevolently persecute believers of a successive move of God. Historically, many of the laborers in a former move become the enemies of the next move because they begin to deify and worship the traditions and teaching pertinent to that move instead of worshiping the God their teachings proclaim.

"FALSE CIRCUMCISION" Refers to counterfeit *spiritual "Jews"*; that is to say, counterfeit Christians.

TRUE, VALID WORSHIP REQUIRES ESTABLISHMENT IN TRUTH

Jn. 4:23 "WHO WORSHIP IN THE SPIRIT": Jesus said, **"The true worshipers shall worship the Father in the Spirit and in Truth; for such people the Father seeks to be His worshipers. God is Spirit, and those who worship Him MUST worship in SPIRIT and in TRUTH."**

"IN SPIRIT" We must worship God through the Holy Spirit's help. Mere forms of carnal religious worship is not acceptable to God. Only Holy Spirit engendered worship is acceptable to God.

> Worshiping God through **ALL** of the fruit and gifts of the Spirit is essential. To resist or reject any of the attributes or manifestations of the Spirit **(1 Cor. 12:7)** is to reject the Holy Spirit Himself.
>
> **1 Thes. 5:19,20 "Do not quench (suppress or subdue) the (Holy) Spirit. Do not spurn the gifts and utterances of the prophets—do not depreciate prophetic revelations nor despise inspired instruction or exhortation or warning."** (Amp. Bible)
>
> Suppressing, discrediting, subduing, undermining, or disallowing prophetic operations is **"QUENCHING THE SPIRIT." It is resisting and quenching the working of the Holy Spirit, the Third Person of the God-Head.**

"WORSHIP...IN TRUTH": Jesus declared Himself to be "the way, the **TRUTH,** and the Life." He was the Word made flesh. Jesus is the embodiment of Truth. Jesus is the Word of God. "Thy Word is Truth" **(Jn. 17:17).** Thus, to reject any portion of Truth that has been revealed as such, is to reject Jesus Himself, for He is Truth.

2 Pet. 1:12 God wants every believer as well as the corporate Body of Christ to be established in present Truth, for to be established in Truth is to be conformed into the image of Christ **(Rom. 8:29)** because Truth is a Person—Christ Himself.

SECTION V: THE COMING RESTORATION AND PURIFICATION

HEB. 1:1 GOD IS NOW SPEAKING *"IN HIS SON"*.

The prophets of the Old Covenant era spoke **"OF"** the Son who was to come. Prophets today are Born Again believers who have been baptized into the Body of Christ and are members of it. They prophesy **"IN"** the Son. New Testament Prophets are **"IN CHRIST"** and are **HIS** hands extended.

Eph. 4:7-11 When He was ascending on High to sit down at the right hand of the Father, Jesus distributed His giftings unto believers for the equipping of believers for effective ministry and for the edification of the Church.

To reject any of these ministry giftings and offices is to reject Jesus himself, for they are part of Him.

1 Cor. 12:27 "Now are we the body of Christ." (See also, **1 Cor. 6:15** and **Eph. 6:30**.)

1 Cor. 12:27,28 Those who function in these ministry appointments have been set in the church and are part of the body of Christ. To reject any of them is to reject Jesus Himself, for they are part of the Body of Christ.

We must receive all that God is doing! If Jesus is doing it, we must receive it and not resist it.

If it's in the Bible—it is Truth! If it is Truth, you know Jesus is doing it.

BY *FAITH* RECEIVING TRUTH AND REJECTING *FEAR* OF DECEPTION

Believers must always receive Truth, and never fear it!

The prophetic realm is a part of Jesus and of Divine Truth. Thus, we must not fear it.

2 Tim. 1:7 Fear is a spirit, not given to us by God.

1 Jn. 4:1-6 Believers need not fear deceiving spirits—they have already overcome them. **Fear is the opposite of faith and produces the opposite results of faith!** Faith is a real spiritual force of the Kingdom of God that produces those things that are desired. Whereas, fear is a real spiritual force of the kingdom of Satan that produces those things that are **not** desired. Job said, **"The thing I have FEARED the most has come upon me."**

FEAR OF DECEPTION will not **protect** us from deception, but will actually **produce** it. **FAITH in God** is our only true protection against evil and deception. Jesus said to pray this way, **"Our Father, which art in Heaven...deliver us from evil."**

"My people are destroyed for LACK OF KNOWLEDGE." Ignorance is not bliss, but stupid. Ignorance or ignoring something is no safeguard against deception. Knowledge does not destroy, **LACK of knowledge** does.

KNOWLEDGE OF THE TRUTH is the only thing that will protect you from deception. Familiarity with the true is the only thing that will protect us from accepting counterfeits. One of the best illustrations of that truth may be **U.S. Treasury Employees**, who handle

A Biblical Perspective of the Prophetic Gifts and Office

genuine bills all day every day. They can spot a counterfeit in a second, just by the feel of it, because they handle so many millions of the genuine.

2 Thes. 3:7-12 LOVE AND ACCEPTANCE OF THE TRUTH is the only safeguard against deception and seduction by false signs and wonders. Those who refuse to become informed about and matured in the use of spiritual gifts will be more and more vulnerable to deception and false signs and wonders.

SUPERNATURAL GIFTS FROM GOD ARE THE GENUINE—THE REAL THING! Supernatural gifts originated with God, not the devil. **Satan is the one who counterfeits the genuine gifts of God, not the other way around!**

Shying away from or resisting the prophetic realm because of fear of deception is itself deception.

To Satan, NEUTRALIZATION IS VICTORY! DISCOURAGEMENT and RETREAT is tantamount to DEFEAT with the devil. If Satan can merely discourage believers from utilizing some of the "weapons of their warfare, which are not carnal, but which are divinely powerful for the pulling down of (Satanic) strongholds," then he has in effect **WON**.

THE PROPHETIC IS PART AND PARCEL OF THE TRUTH

1 Cor. 14:29 LET THE PROPHETS SPEAK. Prophets especially must be permitted to speak Divinely inspired messages.

1 Cor. 14:40 LET ALL THINGS (SPIRITUAL MANIFESTATIONS) BE DONE (OPERATED) IN ACCORDANCE WITH PROPRIETY AND ORDER. Scripture clearly mandates that all of the gifts of the Spirit should be in operation in churches along with the requirement that they be operated according to proper "order."

1 Cor. 14:1, 39 "EARNESTLY DESIRE SPIRITUAL GIFTS"—ESPECIALLY PROPHESYING. Believers should especially earnestly desire to prophesy, above all the other gifts.

1 Cor. 14:22,24; Num. 11:29 Prophesying is for all believers.

1 Cor. 12:31 Earnestly desire the greater gifts. Paul, through the Holy Spirit, establishes here the fact that among the manifestation gifts, some are "greater" than others. There are three categories of manifestation gifts: vocal (Prophetic), Power, Faith, listed in the order of their preeminence. Then, within each category there is an order of preeminence.

1 Cor. 14:1,5 PROPHECY is the GREATEST manifestation gift.

1 Cor. 14:24 THE FRUIT OF PROPHESYING BEARS OUT ITS VALUE AND PREEMINENCE:

1) unbelieving convicted of sin
2) sinners are called to accountability to God
3) secrets of heart disclosed
4) repentance (fall on face)
5) worship of God (exalts Jesus)

A Biblical Perspective of the Prophetic Gifts and Office

SECTION VI:

THE

PROPHETIC GIFTS

AND

OFFICE

LESSON 18
GIFTS VS. OFFICES

MAJOR DIFFERENCES BETWEEN THE "GIFTS" AND "OFFICES"

The Body of Christ needs to understand the crucial differences between the "gifts" and "offices." If one were to attempt to play the game of baseball by the rules of basketball, he would be in big trouble. That is precisely what the Body of Christ has been doing in regards to the "gifts" and "offices."

THREE DIFFERENT CATEGORIES OF GIFTS, EACH FROM A DIFFERENT MEMBER OF THE GOD-HEAD

1 Cor. 12:4-6 This verse explicitly reveals that there are three distinct categories of spiritual giftings, each bestowed by and emanating from a different member of the God-Head:

"Now there are varieties of **GIFTS**, but the same *SPIRIT*. And there are varieties of **MINISTRIES**, but the same *LORD*. And there are varieties of **OPERATIONS** [KJV], but the same *GOD* who works all these things...."

The revelation of this passage is that each member of the God-head has a different set of gifts that emanate from Him and which He distributes to believers. The **Holy Spirit** gives **MANIFESTATION GIFTS (Charismatic Gifts)** for supernatural enablement to be His witnesses, which are delineated in **1 Corinthians 12:7-11**. The Lord **Jesus** Christ as Head of the Church distributes His **MINISTRY GIFTS** for the spiritual development and for the government of the Church, which are listed in **Ephesians 4:7-13**. And, **God the Father** bestows **FUNCTION** or **MOTIVATION** gifts to energize every believer with a specific spiritual function, which are delineated in **Romans 12:4-8**.

ONE PURPOSE OF THE CHARISMATIC MOVE—REDISCOVERY OF "CHARISMATA"

The powerful Wind of the Spirit that began to blow in the sixties and continued until recently, which became known as the **"Charismatic Move,"** not only brought forth a desperately needed "time of refreshing" **(Ac. 3:19)** from the presence of the Lord, but it was also a sovereignly produced, foreordained "period of restoration" **(Ac. 3:21)** by God, in which a "recovery" and a "rediscovery" of the nine "manifestations of the Spirit" (also referred to as "the charismata" or "charismatic gifts") listed in **1 Corinthians 12:7-11** was effected. Thank God for the Charismatic Movement! God's people learned that the manifestations of the Spirit were not merely relegated to some by-gone era of long ago, but that "Jesus Christ is the same today, yesterday, and forever" **(Heb. 13:8)**, and that God changes not **(Mal. 3:6)**! What He was—He is, and what He is—He always will be! For He is God the Eternal and Eternally God! The rediscovery of the manifestations of the Spirit demonstrated once again that it was not God who had changed over the centuries of Church history, but the Church, or perhaps more appropriately, **the doctrines** taught within the Church.

Believers learned in the Charismatic Move that the manifestations of the Spirit, are not just operable through an exclusive group of elite "special people" or just those in Fivefold Minis-

A Biblical Perspective of the Prophetic Gifts and Office

try, but also through ordinary believers. The Lord demonstrated during that movement that the manifestations of the Spirit are indeed just that—manifestations of the **SPIRIT**—not any man, for it is **the Holy Spirit** who "distribute(s) to **EACH ONE** as **HE wills,**" and the Holy Spirit demonstrated that it is His **"will"** to manifest Himself through any believer who will allow Him to do so.

THE FUNCTION OF THE CHARISMATIC GIFTS

The Charismatic Wind came to activate believers who would believe and receive the Holy Spirit and His manifestation gifts in the operation of His supernatural power. The effect of the Baptism in the Holy Spirit, the promise of the Father **(Ac. 1:4,5)**, which Jesus bestows upon every believer who will but ask Him **(Mat. 3:11, Lk. 11:13)**, is that "when the Holy Spirit has come upon you, you will receive **POWER to TESTIFY** about me with great effect" **(Ac. 1:8, L.B.)**. It is **"POWER"** to be **"witnesses"** of Jesus to a lost and dying world that is bestowed upon us when we receive the Baptism in the Holy Spirit.

The Greek word translated "power" in this text is **"dunamis,"** which means **"supernatural enablement."** Thus, the import of Jesus' statement is that with the Baptism of the Holy Spirit we receive supernatural enablement to be vessels for the manifestations of the Spirit through us in order to give testimony of the viability of the resurrection power of Jesus! Upon being endowed with power from on high, we become witnesses of Jesus primarily to the world.

ANOTHER PURPOSE OF THE CHARISMATIC MOVE—MOTIVATION GIFTS

Another major emphasis of the Charismatic Movement was the truth that every believer has a vital place of function in the Body of Christ. There was extensive teaching in Charismatic churches concerning the motivation gifts which emphasized the fact that every individual believer has a function in the Body. Every believer has a primary motivation gift which "energizes" him for **service** unto others. That was a valid and important rediscovery, the full application of which we have yet to see in most churches; albeit, the seed has been planted and we will see the greatest application of this truth toward the end of the present move when the Elisha anointing falls upon the Church.

"CHARISMANIACAL" ERROR

The purposes of God were, of course (because His purposes cannot be denied), fulfilled by the Charismatic Move. At the same time, however, as is often the case in such restorational moves, knowledge came to be exceeded by zeal **(Rom. 10:2)**. As we earnestly attempted to ride the billowing restorational waves of the Charismatic Movement, a kind of "Charismania" or Charismatic error also developed. The spiritual atmosphere of great zeal that happily accompanied the Charismatic Movement also caused an attitude to begin to develop in the minds of some which exceeded what is written **(1 Cor. 4:6)**. As Christians began to understand that they could operate the supernatural "power" of God, some began to mistakenly equate that **"power"** with **AUTHORITY**! Potentially deceiving slogans such as "Well, we are **ALL ministers**" began to emerge. That, of course, is true in the intended sense of the word which is translated alternatingly in the New Testament as "minister" and "servant." We are indeed all **servants** of the Lord, whom the Lord desires to use.

DIFFERENCE BETWEEN POWER AND AUTHORITY

Unfortunately, there is such lack of knowledge among many believers concerning the critical difference between **"power"** and **"authority."** It is imperative that believers understand that "power" to be a witness of Christ is an entirely different matter than **"governmental authority"** within the Church. Many "Charismaniacs" produced in the Charismatic Move did not understand that, and merely because they prayed for someone and God answered by a display of His supernatural power, they began to "think more highly of themselves than they ought" **(Rom. 12:3)**, and some even began to think that they were on par with their appointed spiritual leaders.

Power manifested through operation of the manifestation gifts of the Spirit in no way implies authority to govern within the Church. Power is not the same thing as authority. Power does not supersede or override authority, but rather authority is of a higher level than power. Evidence of this truth is found in Jesus' statement concerning the believer's authority over the power of the devil in **Luke 10:19**: "Behold, I have given you **AUTHORITY** to tread upon serpents and scorpions, and over all the **POWER** of the enemy...." Jesus stated explicitly that Satan does have some **"power,"** contrary to the absurd teaching of some preachers who insist that he does not. Satan does indeed have "power" because it was given to him by Adam, but by virtue of Jesus' triumph over all the powers of hell believers have been given something of a higher level in the spiritual realm than the mere power which Satan possesses—judicial **AUTHORITY**! In Jesus' parting charge to the Church prior to His ascension to occupy His throne, He declared emphatically and categorically that **"ALL AUTHORITY"** both in Heaven and on Earth had been given unto Him, and it was based on and because of that authority that He then charged all believers to exercise that spiritual judicial authority, to wit:

"Go **therefore** into all the world and preach the gospel to all creation, and make disciples of all the nations, baptizing them in the Name of the Father and the Son and the Holy Spirit, teaching them to observe all that I commanded you. He who has believed and has been baptized shall be saved; but he who has disbelieved shall be condemned. And these signs will accompany those who have believed: in My Name they will cast out demons, they will speak with new tongues; they will cast off serpents, and if they drink any deadly poison, it shall not hurt them; they will lay hands on the sick, and they will recover." (Composite of portions of **Mat. 28:18-20** and **Mark 16:15-18**)

It is important to note that while **Chapter 12 of First Corinthians** expounds upon and encourages the operation of the manifestations of the Spirit, the **Fourteenth Chapter** of the same book explains the ground rules by which those gifts must be operated, in order that, as the last verse summarizes, "all things be done properly and in **ORDER**." Everything in the Kingdom of God operates through **Divine Order**, including the governing of the Church. The Church is governed not by those through whom the manifestation gifts of power operate, but by those through whom the governing gifts of authority operate, which are the Fivefold Ministry Officers. While it is true that we are all **ministers of the power of God and the message of Good News, ALL** believers are **NOT Fivefold Ministers. Ephesians 4:11** explicitly states that only **"SOME"**—not **"ALL"**—have been bestowed with Fivefold Ministry gifting. **1 Corinthians 12:28-30** also makes it clear that not all are apostles, prophets, teachers, workers of miracles and gifts of healings (evangelists), and so on.

A Biblical Perspective of the Prophetic Gifts and Office

SECTION VI: THE PROPHETIC GIFTS AND OFFICE

MINISTRY OFFICES

Eph. 4:7-11 "But to each one of us **GRACE** was given according to the measure of Christ's **GIFT**. Therefore it says when He ascended on high...He gave **GIFTS** to men....And He **GAVE** some as apostles, and some as prophets, and some as evangelists, and some as pastors and teachers."

These verses delineate the Fivefold ministry offices that Jesus Himself as the Head of the Body bestowed as a **GIFT** to the Body of Christ. The word in the original language translated as **"grace"** in the above passage is **"charis"** which refers to those **"giftings"** which Christ bestowed to each of us by way of undeserved favor. **Romans 12:6** and **1 Peter 4:10** both indicate that we all have been given certain spiritual **"gifts"** which we are encouraged to employ in servitude unto others. However, this text explicitly states that these particular Fivefold Ministry Office giftings which it lists have been given only to **"SOME"** – particular, selected individuals – not **ALL** believers.

1 Cor. 12:5 Paul informed us in this passage that the gifts the Lord Jesus gives are **"ministry gifts."** In the above text, those gifts are specifically listed as being: apostles, prophets, evangelists, pastors, and teachers **(v. 11)**. In other words, Paul is revealing by the Spirit that when Jesus ascended on High He delegated His authority for building, equipping, and governing within the Church unto those whom He would personally choose, call, anoint, and appoint unto these Ministry Offices. Those whom He so appoints become His personal fleshly delegates to fulfill these building and instructive functions within the Church. This is one of the major differences between the **gifts** and **offices**. Another involves the matter of governmental authority.

THE GOVERNMENT IS UPON JESUS' SHOULDERS (Fivefold MINISTERS)

Is. 9:6 While it is true that every believer is a viable member of and has a vital function in the Body, nevertheless, the Body is still governed through Headship. The **"GOVERNMENT shall be upon His (Jesus') SHOULDERS,"** and the Fivefold Ministry Officers are the New Testament counterpart to the Old Testament Levites upon whose shoulders the Ark of the presence of God (the anointing or authority of God) was to be carried **(Deut. 10:8, 1 Chron. 15:2)**. Fivefold ministry, in addition to having building and instructive responsibility are also the Lord's chosen governing delegates unto the Church.

Eph. 5:23 Despite the claims to sovereignty made by some bureaucratic potentates in man-made religious organizational hierarchies, Jesus Christ Himself is the functioning Head of the Church. He is the only One who is worthy to be its Head. He bought and paid for the Church with His Own shed blood.

Mk. 16:19 After completing His mission of redemption, Jesus Himself ascended into Heaven and sat down at the right hand of God. This phraseology chosen by the Holy Spirit indicates that in ascending into Heaven and sitting down upon His throne, Jesus Himself had accomplished all that He came to accomplish, and that His personal ministry in the flesh had ceased. While He is the **Head** of the Body, **WE** are the **Body**. As Paul said, "Now are **YOU** Christ's body, and individually members of it" **(1 Cor. 12:27)**. We are Jesus' **shoulders**, arms, hands, feet, eyes, ears, and mouth. The Fivefold ministers (the shoulders) are also a part of the Body of Christ. Jesus, the Head of the Body, employs His governing authority through His governmental ambassadors – Fivefold Ministers.

A Biblical Perspective of the Prophetic Gifts and Office

SUMMARY We have seen that some of the major differences between **gifts** and **offices** is that **every** believer has been given a primary **motivation** gift, which he should employ in serving others, and **any** willing believer can be a vessel through whom the Holy Spirit operates the **manifestation** gifts as He wills, but only **some** are anointed by Jesus with **ministry** gifts and set into those offices. Additionally, gifts of the Spirit, while they are manifestations of God's **power**, they do not entail governmental **authority**, as do the ministry gift offices.

Thus far, we have discussed some of the differences between the gifts and offices in general. In the next two lessons, we will see the differences between gifts and offices in terms of the prophetic realm in particular, that is to say, the differences between the simple *gift* of **PROPHECY** and the ministry gift and *office* of the **PROPHET**.

A Biblical Perspective of the Prophetic Gifts and Office

LESSON 19
THE MINISTRY OF THE PROPHET

HEB. 1:1,2 GOD NOW SPEAKS THRU JESUS-APPOINTED MINISTERS

In this New Testament age, God now speaks through His Son, Jesus, who has been installed as the functional Head of the Church. As the Head, Jesus relegated His authority and anointing unto certain people whom He has chosen and ordained to minister on His behalf.

This passage by no means, as some theologians purport, eliminates the office of the Prophet, but on the contrary establishes it under the Headship of Jesus for the duration of the Church Age. If this verse was saying that God only speaks through Jesus now, then **ALL** the ministry offices would have been eliminated, not just the office of the prophet, and **ALL** person-to-person ministry on the human level would be unauthorized.

Eph. 4:7-11 After receiving "all authority in heaven and in earth," Jesus Himself, on the Day of Ascension, as He ascended on high in order to **"SIT DOWN"** at the right hand of the Father, transferred His anointing and authority unto men, thereby creating the Fivefold ministry offices of **Apostles, Prophets,** evangelists, pastors, and teachers.

If you eliminate any of these offices, you must eliminate them all, for they are all found in the same verse. But, nowhere does Scripture say that any of these ministry offices are no longer operable or no longer functioning in the New Testament Church. In fact, it was **AFTER** Jesus had completed His fleshly ministry and ascended into Heaven that all of the ministry offices were established.

The Church Age began with **ALL** ministry offices functioning, and they will continue to be functioning and vital to the spiritual development of the Church, **"UNTIL** we **ALL** attain to the unity of the faith and the knowledge of the Son of God unto a **MATURE MAN"** – until the Church reaches full **MANHOOD** unto the measure of Christ Jesus Himself **(vv. 12,13).**

1 COR. 12:28 APOSTLES AND PROPHETS PERMANENTLY SET IN THE CHURCH

"**GOD** has **SET** in the Church, *first* **APOSTLES**, *second* **PROPHETS**...."

"GOD" Notice first of all that this whole matter of Apostles and Prophets being set into the Church was God's idea, not any man's, nor some apostle's or prophet's trying to promote his own ministry; it originated with God. God did not consult man in the matter of how He was going to build His Church. Contrary to the philosophy of some purported believers, the Church is **not** a **democracy** that is operated in accordance with *"Robert's Rules of Order for Parliamentary Procedure,"* rather it is a *theocracy* operated in accordance with *GOD'S rules of order.* And, God has chosen to build His Church by using Apostles and Prophets as the "master-builders" (we would call them "general-contractors" today) **[1 Cor. 3:10]**.

"SET" Refers to permanence, to set as concrete; immutable, unchangeable.

A Biblical Perspective of the Prophetic Gifts and Office

"IN THE CHURCH" Apostles and **Prophets** have been permanently established **within the Church** by God Himself as preeminently vital ministries, for the duration of the **Church Age**, and are an integral part of all God is doing on planet earth.

Eph. 4:11-13 Prophets have not been dispensationally depleted nor cemented into a non-functional foundation as some theologians contend, but rather they are a vital part of all God has done and shall ever do in His eternal plan for man. This is made clear in **verse 13**, which indicates that **ALL** of the Fivefold Ministry Offices will continue to function in their role of building and instructing—"until"—the collective **"we"** of the true Body of Christ has come into **full maturity** and into **full unity of doctrine**, that is, **"unity of the faith and knowledge of the Son of God."** The Living Bible translates this portion like this: **"until we all believe alike."**

It is the combined task and function of **all** the Fivefold Ministry working in tandem together to bring the Body of Christ to that place of full maturity "unto the measure of the stature of Christ." "Three-Fold" ministry of Evangelists, Pastors, and Teachers, simply cannot get us there. It requires the effectual ministry of Apostles and Prophets in addition to the other three to bring the Church to that place of maturity, both individually and collectively. Until we get to that place, the ministry of the Apostles and Prophets along with the other Fivefold Ministry Offices will be vitally necessary and functioning.

EPH. 2:20 APOSTLES AND PROPHETS ARE THE *FOUNDATIONAL MINISTRIES* OF THE CHURCH

The ministries of the Apostles and Prophets are the foundational ministries upon which the Church is built. Without the ministry of Apostles and Prophets the revelation of the "blueprint" and the "gifting" necessary to build the building is incomplete. Without the ministry of the Apostles and Prophets (who are directly connected to the Cornerstone [Christ Jesus]) being in place and functioning, the framework of the building will be askew and out of plumb, which is precisely the present condition of the Church.

DEFINING THE MINISTRY OF PROPHETS—God's Communication Channels

The Prophet—God's spokesman: from "pro" = on behalf of / "phet" = to speak. Simply defined, the Prophet is God's spokesman. The Prophet is a Fivefold Minister who has been set apart, appointed, and anointed with the ministry gifting of a Prophet, and has been permanently set into that office. Though every believer has a vital function he has been anointed and appointed by the Lord to perform, it must be understood that no amount of zeal, enthusiasm, fervor, prayer, or even Bible study, can vaunt a person into **any ministry office**, including that of **Prophet**. It is only the appointing and anointing of the Lord that makes a prophet a prophet. Fivefold ministry starts with a **calling**, not a desire, and that calling must be from God. Your mother, your father, or your wife cannot call you to the ministry; you can't even call yourself; **only God** can call a person to the ministry.

True **prophets** are not **novices**, neither are they mere aspiring ministers. A true **prophet** is not someone trying to become a prophet, he **IS** one. While "schools of prophets" can be helpful in developing those that have been anointed by God with the anointing of a prophet, one cannot simply take a course to **"learn"** to be a prophet. No one can really **"teach"** someone to be a prophet. Prophets are **not "taught,"** but are usually **"caught"** and then **"made"** by the Lord. No one can **intrude** into any ministry office successfully, especially the office of the prophet. We describe the ministry offices merely for the sake of understanding them better, but merely calling yourself something, whether it be: "a prophet," or "a teacher," or "a '56Oldsmobile," for that matter, does not make you one. Any minister is what he is because of what he does, not because of what he calls himself. The best approach for any minister is to simply do all that God has equipped him and allows him to do, and let that define his office.

The **office of the Prophet** and the **"one who prophesies"** (1 Cor. 14:3,5) are two distinct functions with vast differences separating them. **"One who prophesies"** can be **any willing believer** through whom the Holy Spirit chooses to operate the simple manifestation **gift of prophecy**. The **office of the prophet**, however, is only given to **"some"** (Eph. 4:11), that is to say, certain God-selected individuals, who God has anointed with supernatural enablement to minister in a building and instructive capacity. The fact that one is merely used by God to **prophesy** does not make that person a **prophet** by any means. Another major difference is that the simple gift of prophecy by a lay-believer (non-Fivefold Minister) must be limited to edification, exhortation, and comfort, while the ministry of a **prophet** is not so limited, but in addition to these may also include: revelation, illumination, foretelling of future events, divine counsel, guidance, direction, correction, admonition, and in some extreme cases, even rebuke.

DIFFERENT KINDS OF PROPHETS

There are many different kinds of prophets. It is just as incorrect to stereotype prophets as it is to say that all pastors or evangelists, for example, are the same. God made us all different.

We all have different personalities, talents, and abilities that God has given us. All ministers do not have the same calling or emphasis of ministry. This is just as true for prophets. Jeremiah, for example, was called the "weeping prophet," while Ezra, Nathan, and Gad were "writing prophets," the latter two of which wrote 2 Samuel and 1 & 2 Chronicles.

There are prophets who are also teachers (**Ac. 13:1**).

There are prophets whose primary ministry is within a local body (**1 Cor. 12:28**). Some prophets are called to be the local resident apostle over a work, giving it apostolic oversight. Yet, other prophets have a traveling ministry, and some are sent out to function not only as prophets but also as apostles (**Acts 13:1-4**).

THE FUNCTION OF PROPHETS

Jer. 1:10 In this verse God delineates the six primary functions of the prophet. The six-faceted ministry of the prophet can be summed up with the following descriptions:

1) **to pluck (root) up**—"weeds," both in the lives of individual believers, as well as "weeds" growing in the Church, which is false teaching and false brethren.
2) **to break down**—resistances and rebellion to God's Word, Will, and Way by believers.
3) **to destroy**—vain philosophies and imaginations raised up against the knowledge of God; and, Satan's works.
4) **to overthrow**—the kingdoms of men; and strongholds of the devil.
5) **to build**—the Church at-large and local churches, spiritually upon the foundation of the purposes and Life of Christ.
6) **to plant**—Christ as the Seed of God in the Church and in the individual lives of believers; and, along with Apostles—plant Churches.

A Biblical Perspective of the Prophetic Gifts and Office

The following are some of the functions of prophets which can be deduced from the composite of many different Scriptures far too numerous to list individually.

>Reveal **the mind of Christ** and **give specific instruction** concerning His personal **will** for the lives of individuals as well as for groups.
>
>Unveil **revelation** and **illumination** and **inspired application** of the Logos.
>
>Give **confirmation and witness** in various ways through their ministry.
>
>Relate **divine direction** to the Church and churches.
>
>Elicit **repentance, reformation,** and **restoration**.

The following are some functions of prophets with a specific Scripture citing to support them:

>**Amos 3:7** **Prophets** are given the secret counsel of God.
>
>**1 Sam. 9:9** **Prophets** are SEERS — they see things supernaturally in the Spirit that other people don't see.
>
>**Jer. 18:18; 2 Kgs. 6:8-12** **Prophets** are HEARERS — they can hear supernaturally, when God allows them, the speech of others that are not intended to be heard by others, such as slander spoken against themselves and covert evil plans conceived in secrecy.
>
>**Jer. 1:16,17** **Prophets** pronounce judgment
>
>**Eph. 4:11-13** **Prophets** perfect, mature, Saints and the Church to Manhood.
>
>**Rev. 11:3-13** **Prophets** will execute God's judgments.
>
>**Prophets** expose sin:
>
>>**Eph. 5:11** Exposure of sin is a Divine charge.
>>
>>**Jn. 4:7-19** Jesus, a **Prophet**, exposed the sin of the Samaritan woman.
>>
>>**Mat. 23** Jesus, a **Prophet**, exposed the sin of the Pharisees.
>>
>>**Mk. 6:18** John the Baptist, a **Prophet**, exposed the sin of Herod.
>>
>>**Ac. 13:10,11** **Prophet** Paul **(Ac. 13:1)** exposed sin and brought temporal judgment upon Elymas the magician.
>>
>>**Ac. 16:16** **Prophet** Paul exposes the sin of witchcraft in a fortune-teller.
>>
>>**Gal. 2:11-13** *Prophet* Paul exposed *Apostle* Peter's sin of hypocrisy.
>>
>>**2 Sam. 11:1 - 12:13** Nathan the **Prophet** exposed the sin of David.
>>
>>**2 Kgs. 5:26** Elisha the **Prophet** exposed the sin of his servant.

THE END-TIME ELIJAH COMPANY OF PROPHETS WILL ACCOMPLISH THE FINAL PURPOSES OF THE LORD

THE ELIJAH COMPANY OF PROPHETS presently being raised up by the Lord will fulfill these prophecies — they will:

Prepare the way for the SECOND COMING of Christ — Is. 40:3

Make ready a people (The Church) prepared for the Lord — Lk. 1:17; Rev. 19:7,8; Rev. 21:2; Eph. 4:11-13; Eph. 5:25-27

Transform the Church into "An exceedingly Great Army" — Ezk. 37:1-14

Rev. 10:7; 11:15 The ministry of the **COMPANY OF PROPHETS** will bring the **culmination of the Church Age**.

Acts 3:21 When the **prophets** have finished their ministry, **Christ will be released** to return to claim His Church-Bride.

END-TIME COMPANY OF JUDGMENT PROPHETS

Prior to the return of Christ, God will bring forth a company of prophets who will be His threshing sledge and winnowing fork in His hand **(Is. 41:16; Mat. 3:12)** to execute this judgment of the household of God, which will be the final separation of the wheat from the chaff. **They are coming,** and believers and ministers alike must begin to adjust their attitudes and allow their minds to be enlightened by what the Bible has to say about these very necessary and valid ministries, lest they find themselves fighting against the very plans and purposes of God, and therefore — God Himself.

Until now, the Lord has tolerated a lot within the Body of Christ that He does not intend to tolerate forever. Judgment within "the household of God" (the Church) will precede judgment of the world **(1 Pet. 4:17)**. Thus, He is gradually bringing forth His prophets to a place of real function in which they will be performing without constraint (save that of the true nature of the love of God) the six-faceted ministry of prophets, i.e., to: 1) pluck up, 2) break down, 3) destroy, 4) overthrow, 5) build, and 6) plant **(Jer. 1:10)**.

Just as God raised up **Elijah** to bring to nought the influence of the false prophets of Baal, so also shall He bring forth **prophets of power and judgment** within the Church who will cause the kingdom of God on the earth to "suffer violence" as they exert the authority of God, in some cases by spiritual force, over entities and elements within the domain of God which have been resistant to the will and purposes of God. They shall function in tandem with the apostles that God will have also raised up, and some of these prophets will also themselves be apostles as well, with apostolic function. The end-time genuine apostles and prophets will be used of God to bring forth His ultimate end-time purposes and plans in a measure and by means that shall be unprecedented in the history of the Church as well as the world. There shall be an unprecedented release of supernatural power released in and through them to perform tasks and assignments absolutely vital to the end-time purposes and plans of God. God shall consign unto these tried and tested vessels an unction of spiritual authority that shall be like unto Moses in his function as the delieverer of Israel from Egypt bondage and Elijah in his function as the destoryer and avenger of false religion and idol worship.

A Biblical Perspective of the Prophetic Gifts and Office

LESSON 20
THE GIFT OF PROPHECY

FOUNDATION SCRIPTURE: 1 COR. 12, 13, 14

PRESENT TRUTH IS EVER EVOLVING UNTIL PERFECT (KNOWLEDGE) COMES

"...and be established in the **PRESENT TRUTH**." **(1 Pet. 1:12)**

"**...as for knowledge**, it will pass away [that is, it will lose its value and **be superseded by truth**]. For our knowledge is fragmentary (incomplete and imperfect), and our prophecy (our teaching) is fragmentary (incomplete and imperfect). **But when the complete and perfect [total] comes, the incomplete and imperfect will vanish away — become antiquated, void and superseded.** When I was a child, I talked like a child, I thought like a child, I reasoned like a child; now that I have become a man, I am done with childish ways and have put them aside. For now we are looking in a mirror that gives only a dim (blurred) reflection [of reality as in a riddle or enigma], but then [when perfection comes] we shall see in reality and face to face! **Now I know in part (imperfectly); but then I shall know and understand fully and clearly,** even in the same manner as I have been fully and clearly known and understood [by God]." **(First Corinthians 13:8-12, Amplified Bible)**

The entrance of God's Word gives light, or illumination of the Truth **(Ps. 119:130).** By and by, throughout the ages, God has been dispelling spiritual darkness in the Church by gradually revealing more and more Truth and by gradually giving us greater illumination of the Truth. As a result the Church's understanding of the Truth is becoming more and more complete and perfected. This is what the Holy Spirit means in His allusion to being "established in **present Truth**." Certainly it is not that the Truth of God changes or needs up-dating, but rather this refers to the Church's **understanding** of the Truth. This process seems to be especially accelerated in these last days in which much fresh Truth is being revealed to the Church through a "new breed" of Fivefold Ministers.

As the above Scripture (especially in the Amplified Bible's paraphrase) indicates, partial and incomplete knowledge is continuously being superseded by more complete and perfect knowledge through the revelation of new illumination of the Truth. As we move closer toward the coming of perfect knowledge, it may now be that God is revealing fresh illumination of the Truth regarding the subject of the "manifestations of the Spirit" as well, especially the **prophetic** gifts. The Charismatic Movement brought forth a restoration of and renewed awareness in the "charismata gifts" of the Spirit. However, that restoration and renewed awareness was centered primarily around the revelation and power gifts. Though there was sporadic use of the prophetic giftings during that move in some circles, by and large, the prophetic realm was a less explored and expounded upon subject, and the prophetic arm of the Church remained to be neglected, largely undeveloped, and was kept at an arm's distance. This always was a source of great concern to me, and I never could understand why God would allow this to be so year after year after year, knowing all along myself that the prophetic realm and the prophetic arm of the Church was almost a completely untapped resource of tremendous power and strength to the Church. But, it seemed as though this area was a "sealed up" chapter in the book of divine knowledge.

A Biblical Perspective of the Prophetic Gifts and Office

But, how wondrous are the ways of God! After all those years, the Lord has now initiated a new and separate movement in which the prophetic realm is being established within the Church. The winds of restoration of the prophetic realm have already begun to blow throughout the Church, and God is bringing fresh revelation and illumination to the Church concerning this previously neglected area of Truth. Perhaps to some, much of the content of this section will be "new" revelation, while to others it may offer more clarity in regard to the prophetic realm—both are needed.

1 COR. 12:1   INFORMED, NOT IGNORANT

God desires for all believers to be **INFORMED, NOT IGNORANT** concerning the manifestation gifts of the Spirit, just as He desires for us to be informed about every other matter of the Spirit realm. Yet, there is perhaps more ignorance regarding this one matter than any other.

One of the remnants ostensibly of the Dark Ages in the Church which is still prevalent in many churches today is the ridiculous hypothesis that ignorance about spiritual matters perceived by some to be potentially erroneous should be totally avoided and that one should emulate the ostriches and bury his head in the sand so as to not even look upon anything which may be unorthodox or different than the traditional beliefs. Many denominational churches still teach that kind of childish and medieval-like behavior even for their adult church members pertaining to the matter of the baptism in the Spirit and the gifts of the Spirit, and related spiritual matters. Non-pentecostal/charismatic preachers and church leaders admonish their parishioners against becoming involved with Charismatic groups with such foolish statements as "you better stay away from those tongue-talkers and those 'holy-rollers' and those 'snake-handlers' lest some of that what they've got might get on you." The premise of their thinking is that ignorance and avoidance of anything different than the traditional doctrines of that denomination is the way to prevent deception.

Nothing could be further from the Truth! Even the pagan Bereans had more spiritual sense than that, for when they heard the preaching by Paul of "another Way" than what they had known, they "received the word with great eagerness, **examining the Scriptures** daily to see whether these things were so" **(Ac. 17:11)**. The only way to know whether a teaching is true or false is to examine it in the light of Scripture. The deception preventative prescribed by God's Word is to "Test and prove all things [until you can recognize] what is good; to that hold fast" **(1 Thes. 5:21, A.B)**; and the only way we can test and prove any spiritual matter is by comparing it to Holy Scripture. If God's Word says it, then it is so.

As discussed in Lesson 17, ignorance or avoidance of something is no safeguard against deception. God said His people are destroyed because of **"lack of knowledge."** Lack of knowledge, or ignorance, of the Truth is what causes us to be destroyed. Knowledge itself never destroys—lack of knowledge does. It's not even knowledge of the untrue or the erroneous that destroys us, but rather **lack of knowledge** of the Truth! (Note: Though the following comments were presented in the context of Lesson 17, they bear repeating here.)

Believers must always **receive TRUTH** by **FAITH**, and never **FEAR** it! It is FEAR of DECEPTION that we must **reject**. **FEAR OF DECEPTION** will not **protect** us from it, but will only **produce** it. **FAITH in God** is our only true protection against evil and deception. Jesus said to pray this way, **"Our Father, which art in Heaven...deliver us from evil."**

2 Tim. 1:7 **FEAR** is an evil **SPIRIT**, emanating from Satan, not God. **Fear** is the opposite of **faith** and produces the opposite results of faith. **Faith** is a real, effectual spiritual force of the Kingdom of God which produces those things that **are** desired. **Fear** is a real spiritual force of the kingdom of Satan that produces the things that are **not** desired. Job said, **"The thing I have FEARED the most HAS COME UPON ME!"**

1 Jn. 4:1-6 Believers need not fear **DECEIVING SPIRITS**, because we have **ALREADY OVERCOME THEM.**

2 Thes. 3:7-12 Love of and acceptance of the **TRUTH** is the only safeguard against **DECEPTION** and subjection to false signs and wonders. It is those who refuse to become informed about and matured in the matter of spiritual gifts who will be more and more vulnerable to deception and false signs and wonders.

Supernatural gifts from God are the **GENUINE—THE REAL THING!!** Supernatural gifts originated with God, not the devil. Satan is the one who counterfeits the genuine gifts of God, not the other way around! The very existence of the occultic counterfeit signs and wonders is proof-positive of the existence of the genuine supernatural gifts of God.

The **PROPHETIC** realm is **PART AND PARCEL OF JESUS AND DIVINE TRUTH.** Thus, we must not fear it or reject it. Shying away from or resisting the prophetic realm because of fear of deception is itself deception and is precisely what the devil wants to cause believers to do so that they will not use the supernatural weapons of their warfare **(2 Cor. 10:4)** to defeat him and his kingdom. To Satan, neutralization is victory. Discouragement-caused **RETREAT** is tantamount to **DEFEAT**.

1 COR. 12:7 MANIFESTATIONS OF THE SPIRIT—FOR THE COMMON GOOD

The Apostle Paul's entire dissertation in chapters 12, 13, 14 of First Corinthians concerns the nine supernatural "manifestations of the Spirit". All nine of these gifts of the Spirit, according to the above passage, are **FOR THE COMMON GOOD,** that is to say, they are primarily manifested **in the public congregational forum,** for the corporate benefit of those assembled. According to this Scripture, these manifestations are most likely to be manifested in the congregational forum ("where two or three are gathered together in My name") as opposed to the private and personal life of an individual believer.

It is in this public congregational forum that the manifestations of the Spirit are most frequently and commonly manifested and demonstrated. For instance, the working of miracles, the gifts of healings, and faith seem to be activated and manifested more commonly "where two or three are gathered together," for "the **common** good," than they are in the personal life of an individual for the "private" benefit of that individual. This demonstrates the importance of the corporate anointing **(Jn. 14:12).**

The verses immediately following the listing of the manifestations of the Spirit **(1 Cor. 12:12-27)** seem to be focusing upon and emphasizing this matter of these manifestations being especially operational in the corporate Body of Christ, which, though it consists of individual members, is individual members related to and needful of one another and assembled together corporately. "But one and the same Spirit works all these things (the manifestations of the Spirit), distributing to each one individually as He wills." The "will" of the Spirit seems to encompass an especial preference for distributing these manifestations and causing them to operate when the corporate Body of Christ congregates together, reinforcing the Lord's insistence that we be continually cognizant of our need for one another. For instance, while it is possible for a sick believer to lay hands upon himself and produce his recovery, that seems to be a rare occurrence; rather, it seems that healing virtue is more often released into the body of the infirmed through the laying on of hands by another believer.

1 COR. 12:4-6 THREE VARIETIES OF GIFTS, EACH BESTOWED BY A DIFFERENT MEMBER OF THE GOD-HEAD

(v. 6) God The *Father*: MOTIVATION GIFTS (Rom. 12:4-8).

(v. 5) God The *Son*: MINISTRY GIFTS (Eph. 4:7-11).

(v. 4) God The *Holy Spirit*: MANIFESTATION GIFTS (1 Cor. 12:8-10).

GENERAL DEFINITION OF THE MANIFESTATIONS GIFTS

Nine supernatural manifestations operated by the Holy Spirit, through His initiation and inspiration, at His sole discretion, through any willing and obedient believer He wills, to perform His will and purposes for the common good of others.

THE NINE MANIFESTATION GIFTS DIVIDED INTO THREE MAIN CATEGORIES

PROPHETIC GIFTS:
1) Prophecy
2) Diversities of Tongues
3) Interpretation of Tongues

REVELATION GIFTS:
1) Word of Wisdom,
2) Word of Knowledge
3) Discernment of Spirits

POWER GIFTS:
1) Faith
2) Working of Miracles
3) Gifts of Healings

THE PROPHETIC GIFTS ARE THE GREATER GIFTS

1 Cor. 12:31 "But earnestly desire the **greater gifts**."

Among the manifestation gifts of the Spirit, there are **"GREATER"** gifts, that is to say, some gifts have a greater spiritual impact and require a greater anointing to operate than others. The term "greater gifts" also indicates there is an order of ascendency among the three categories of manifestation gifts as well as within each category. In other words, of the three categories of manifestation gifts, some are greater than the others, and each category has an order of importance as well. For example—

1 Cor. 14:5 "and **GREATER** is one who **PROPHESIES** than one who speaks in tongues, unless he interprets...."

This verse presents an example of "greater gifts" within a category of manifestation gifts. According to this verse, among the Vocal Gifts, **prophecy** is the greatest, interpretation of tongues is next, then tongues. Not only is the gift greater, but the "one who prophesies", according to this verse, is operating in a greater level of the anointing than the "one who speaks in tongues." The exception to this is—**"unless he interprets,"** meaning that if the person who speaks the message in tongues also interprets, then he is operating equally in anointing, gifting, and equipping as the "one who prophesies."

1 Cor. 14:1 "Pursue love, yet desire earnestly spiritual gifts, but **ESPECIALLY** that you may **PROPHESY**...."

This passage indicates that **PROPHESY** is to be desired above all the other nine spiritual manifestations of the Spirit. He exhorts believers to **"ESPECIALLY,"** above all the other gifts, covet to **"PROPHESY"**. Because "tongues" with "interpretation of tongues" is equivalent to and is a varied form of "prophecy" (see explanation below), **"Prophecy"** is actually representative of the entire category of the Vocal Gifts. Hence, believers should desire to operate the Vocal Gifts more than all the other manifestation gifts.

1 Cor. 14:5 "Now I wish that you all spoke in tongues, but **EVEN MORE** that you would **PROPHESY**...."

Here the Holy Spirit indicates through the Apostle Paul that He desires for every believer to speak in tongues, but **"EVEN MORE"** that all believers would **"PROPHESY"**. Again we see that **PROPHECY** should be the most desired gift of the Vocal gifts.

1 Cor. 14:1-4 "Pursue love, yet **desire earnestly spiritual gifts,** but **especially** that you may **PROPHESY. FOR...one who prophesies SPEAKS TO MEN for EDIFICATION and EXHORTATION and CONSOLATION...one who prophesies EDIFIES THE CHURCH."**

Believers are exhorted to earnestly desire the operation of the manifestations of the Spirit through their lives. We are exhorted more specifically to **"ESPECIALLY"** desire earnestly the operation of the gift of **prophecy** through us above all the other manifestation gifts. But, it is the word **"FOR"** that is key to this passage, which indicates that the reason for that which has just been stated follows. This word "for" is synonymous with the word "because." The reason cited for the exhortation to desire to prophesy above operation of all the other gifts is that "one who prophesies **speaks to men**," meaning the one who prophesies speaks messages from God to men. The import here is that to speak on behalf of God unto men (prophecy) is the operation of the Spirit that performs the greatest benefit unto the recipients, though it also bears the greatest responsibility unto the one who prophesies.

Beyond that, we are told that further reason for us to "covet to prophesy" even more than we desire to operate any of the other manifestation gifts is because of the surpassing value of the benefits of prophecy, which are: **EDIFICATION, EXHORTATION,** and **COMFORT**. Apparently, the Holy Spirit is telling us here that beyond healing, miracles, and supernatural revelation, the greatest need of believers is to be **edified** (spiritually charged-up as a battery is charged-up), **exhorted** (encouraged, entreated, admonished), and comforted (consoled, cheered up, encouraged).

A Biblical Perspective of the Prophetic Gifts and Office

Despite the invaluable benefit of prophecy to the individual, we are told that there is a surpassing benefit when one prophesies, which is that it **"edifies THE CHURCH."** In other words, when a member of the Church is edified, exhorted, and comforted, the accumulative effect is that the collective Church is edified.

Also The Reason The Devil Despises Prophecy

Once, as I was in prayer in my hotel room just prior to the start of one of my prophetic seminars, I was going over my notes, and as I came to this portion, the Lord said to me, **"This is why the devil hates prophecy so much!"** At the time, though we were having tremendous meetings in which many people were healed, delivered, and greatly ministered to prophetically, we were also the target of some devil-inspired resistance perpetrated by a few insecure preachers and church leaders who were jealous of the stir our meetings were creating. To cover their true motivations, they tried to dissuade their church members from attending the seminars by making statements that served only to demonstrate their ignorance regarding the prophetic realm. The Lord told me they were just pawns of the devil, who was the real perpetrator of the resistance because he **despised prophecy!**

Then, the Lord told me that the reason the devil despises prophecy so much is that **prophecy EDIFIES THE CHURCH**. The last thing that the devil wants is for the Church collectively and its individual members to be spiritually **edified** (charged-up). The devil's power is very limited. His success depends primarily on his ability to deceive and to discourage. He does all he can to keep us from knowing who we really are in Christ and the surpassing power that we have over him and his kingdom. When we begin to understand some of these things, he then does all he can to keep us discouraged and neutralized, which is tantamount to defeat for us and victory for the devil. But, this is the very purpose and benefit of prophecy: to edify, exhort, and encourage us. And, if there has ever been a time when believers need to be edified, exhorted, and encouraged it is the complex and difficult days in which we live today. In light of this it is no wonder that the devil is instigating so much resistance to the prophetic move of God in the Church.

1 COR. 12:10 THE UTTERANCE (VOCAL) GIFTS

The Utterance or Vocal Gifts are one of the three categories of the manifestations of the Spirit, consisting of **prophecy, tongues,** and **interpretation of tongues.** They could also be correctly referred to as the "Prophetic Gifts." It is the Utterance Gifts that are pertinent to this course, and thus our focus of attention.

DEFINING THE MANIFESTATION GIFT OF PROPHECY

1 Cor. 14:3,4 "...**ONE WHO PROPHESIES speaks to men** for **edification** and **exhortation** and **consolation**...**ONE WHO PROPHESIES edifies the church**."

A supernatural, ecstatic, and spontaneous utterance through the unction and inspiration of the Holy Spirit spoken or portrayed through a believer either in the common language of the hearers or in a tongue unknown to the hearers accompanied by an interpretation of the unknown tongues for the common benefit of the hearers.

A Biblical Perspective of the Prophetic Gifts and Office

"Prophesy" means to speak a message on behalf of someone else. In the spiritual sense, it means to speak on behalf of God.

Prophecy is a message from God to a person or a group.

THE FUNCTION AND BENEFITS OF PROPHECY

1 Cor. 14:3,4 "...ONE WHO PROPHESIES speaks to men for edification and exhortation and consolation...ONE WHO PROPHESIES edifies the church."

There are three primary functions of the Manifestation Gift of Prophecy:

1) **edification** — to spiritually charge up as a battery is charged up, spiritually strengthen, to impart;
2) **exhortation** — to advise, admonish, entreat, urge, warn, prompt;
3) **consolation** — to encourage, cheer up, comfort.

THE EFFECTS AND FRUIT OF PROPHECY

1 Cor. 14:22-25 "...but **prophecy** is for a **sign**...to those who believe...But if all **prophesy**, and an **unbeliever** or an **ungifted man** enters, he is **convicted** by all, he is **called to account** by all; **the secrets of his heart are disclosed;** and so he will **fall on his face and worship God, declaring that God is certainly among you.**"

Besides the function of communicating a message from God to edify, exhort, and console a congregation, the purpose of prophecy is to serve as a supernatural **"sign"** especially to **believers.**

There are also six effects listed in the above passages which prophecy (in the common language of the congregation or in foreign tongues with interpretation) is intended to have upon the unbelieving and the "ungifted" (those not baptized in the Holy Spirit):

1) conviction of sin;
2) call to accountability;
3) disclosure of the secrets of the heart;
4) effect godly sorrow, repentance, and submission to God;
5) effect sincere worship of God;
6) effect a recognition of the power of God and His presence in the midst of that assembly of believers.

THE QUESTION OF *WHO* SHOULD PROPHESY

1 Cor. 14:5 "Now I wish that you all spoke in tongues, but **EVEN MORE** that you would **PROPHESY**...."

God desires for **ALL** believers to speak in tongues. But, as much as He desires for all believers to speak in tongues, **"EVEN MORE"** He desires for **ALL** believers to **PROPHESY**. Perhaps, we have had such an emphasis in the Charismatic Movement on all believers availing themselves of their entitlement to speak in tongues that we have underemphasized the fact that God desires even more that all believers would **prophesy.** This notion that all believers can prophesy would admittedly be foreign to many. Nevertheless, it is Scriptural, though obviously it cannot be done at the will of the believer any more than the other gifts can be operated at the will of the believer, but only, we recognize, **"as the Spirit wills."**

This idea may be harmonious with and further supported by another unusual and otherwise puzzling story found in **Numbers 11:24-29**. (Summarizing—)

The Lord came down and took of the Spirit who was upon Moses and placed Him upon the seventy elders.

When the Spirit rested upon them, they prophesied. But they did not do it again.

Two other men—laymen, not among the seventy elders—had remained in the camp—Eldad ("loved of God") and Medad ("would be loving). **The Spirit also rested upon them, and they also prophesied in the camp.**

This was like a "Charismatic Movement" among the Hebrews. To some of Moses' proteges it was blasphemous for these ordinary laymen to be prophesying, and a challenge to Moses' spiritual elitism. Thus, they became indignant, and appealed for Moses to **"restrain them."** But Moses refused to censor or hinder them, saying, "Are you jealous for my sake? **(I) Would that ALL the Lord's people were prophets, that the Lord would put His Spirit upon them!"**

This passage shatters all the "exclusivity" and "elitist" notions held by some regarding the operation of manifestations of the Spirit. It demonstrates categorically that the Holy Spirit can manifest Himself through any willing believer He desires to manifest through, and indeed is an encouragement to every believer to be willing to be used by the Holy Spirit in the manifestation gifts of the Spirit. (NOTE: to be consistent with **1 Cor. 12:29** and other New Testament passages distinguishing between the "gift of prophecy" and the "office of the prophet," the term "prophets" in this passage must allude to **"one who prophesies"**, that is, one who operates the simple gift of prophecy, and not one who has been set in the **office** of a prophet. It does not say that any of those who prophesied when the Spirit came upon them were **"prophets"**, only that they **"prophesied."**)

1 Thes. 5:19,20 "Do not **quench** the Spirit; do not **despise** prophetic utterances."

The command, "Do not quench the Spirit," must primarily be an admonition regarding not quenching the **manifestations** (operation of the gifts) of the Spirit because it would not be possible for any human to literally "quench" the Holy Spirit Himself or to "extinguish" His fire. Man is not capable of "quenching" the Person of the Holy Spirit, but can indeed quench the manifestations of His power through human vessels. The Holy Spirit is a "Gentleman" and never intrudes where He is not honored or wanted.

Verse 20 makes it even more clear that He is talking about quenching the Spirit in the sense of quenching the manifestations of the Spirit. The term "prophetic utterances" would of necessity also include "tongues," because tongues with its required companion of interpretation **IS** prophecy in its varied form.

Though excesses and error have always existed in the operation of the manifestations of the Spirit, we must never "despise prophetic utterances" or the operation of any of the manifestations of the Spirit (apparently God anticipated that this temptation would exist; hence this verse). Moreover, we must resist the temptation to quench the operation of the Spirit, and certainly must not go to the extreme of "forbidding" the operation of the manifestations of the Holy Spirit in our meetings. That would be a far greater "excess" and "error" than the so-called "excesses" and "error" which have been cited by some who needed an excuse to justify their forbidding of the operation of the prophetic gifts in their churches.

The Scriptural thing to do in order to eliminate excesses and error is what the Apostle Paul did at the church at Corinth — teach and train the people in the proper operation of the Spirit and how to "prove all things;" then they will have had their spiritual senses trained to be able "to discern (that which is) good and (that which is) evil" **(Heb. 5:14)**.

1 Cor. 14:39 "But **LET all** things (manifestations of the Spirit) be done properly and in an orderly manner."

This passage instructs that we should allow **ALL** spiritual manifestations to operate in our meetings without hindrance or restriction as long as they are operated according to the prescribed rules of order and propriety. This would include all the vocal gifts as well as all the others.

LESSON 21
THE MANIFESTATION GIFT OF TONGUES

THE MANIFESTATION GIFT OF TONGUES

1 Cor. 12:28 "And **God** has **APPOINTED in the church**...(various) **kinds of tongues.**"

The Manifestation Gift of Tongues defined: a supernatural God-inspired message spoken through a person in a language unknown to the speaker and not commonly known to the hearers, which must be interpreted into the common language of the hearers.

It was God's idea and doing, not man's, to appoint, or set in, the congregation of the church different "kinds of tongues." God has ordained that various kinds of tongues should be operating in the assembly of the Church. No where does Scripture inform us that God has rescinded the appointment of the gift of various forms of tongues in the Church, though many have sought to have them "impeached" from the Church.

FORMULA: TONGUES + INTERPRETATION = PROPHECY

1 Cor. 14:2-5 "For one who speaks in a tongue does not speak to men, but to God; for no one understands, but in his spirit he speaks mysteries. But one who prophesies speaks to men... one who prophesies edifies the church...**and greater is one who PROPHESIES than one who SPEAKS IN TONGUES, *UNLESS HE INTERPRETS*....**"

It is in verse 5 that we find the explanation that **tongues with interpretation is EQUIVALENT to prophecy**. In other words: **TONGUES + INTERPRETATION = PROPHECY**.

Conversely, because tongues **must** be interpreted to be a proper prophetic utterance in the congregational usage, the following would also be an accurate description:

TONGUES - INTERPRETATION = prayer and praise.

TONGUES SHOULD NOT BE HINDERED OR FORBIDDEN:

1 Cor. 14:39 "...do not **forbid** to speak in tongues."

To forbid to speak in tongues, is to forbid **God from speaking,** for tongues is **a message from God** manifested through the Holy Spirit.

No one has authority from the Scripture to forbid the speaking forth of tongues as a God-inspired message from God in a service that is done decently and in order. Those who try to in any way hinder, suppress, restrict, demean, belittle, or stop the free operation of this manifestation of the Spirit, does so against God Himself and the Holy Spirit, since it was God's appointment, or ordination, and since tongues is a manifestation of the Holy Spirit Himself and not of any man. Those who engage in these acts against the Holy Spirit often approach committing and sometimes do commit sin against the Holy Spirit, which Jesus said would never be forgiven **(Mk. 3:28, 29).**

A Biblical Perspective of the Prophetic Gifts and Office

TONGUES USED AS A PRAYER AND PRAISE LANGUAGE:

1 Cor. 14:14,15 "For if I **PRAY** in a tongue, my spirit **PRAYS**, but my mind is unfruitful. What is the outcome then? I shall **PRAY** with the spirit and I shall **PRAY** with the mind also; I shall sing with the spirit and I shall sing with the mind also."

> Though appearing in the context concerning the proper operation of the manifestations of the Spirit in the congregational forum, the above verses **DO NOT** pertain to the manifestation gift of **"SPEAKING"** in tongues, but rather to the personal "prayer and praise language in tongues." These verses and the preceding verse **(v. 13)** are the only times the Greek word **"proseuchomai"** (pray) is used in this **14th Chapter**. The matter of **"praying in the Spirit"** is mentioned here in connection with **verse 13** (note the prefatory word "for" at the beginning of the verse) to illustrate the fact that when a person uses an "unknown tongue" an interpretation is needful because his "mind (intellect) is unfruitful"—in other words, his mind does not understand what has been said in the tongue that is unknown to him. All the rest of the usages of the word "tongues" is in connection with the Greek word "laleo" (speak). The word "speak" carries with it the connotation "to speak **a message.**"

> Instructions pertaining to the orderly operation of "tongues" given in the dissertation of **First Corinthians 12 & 14** are not references to the personal "prayer and praise language" received by believers baptized in the Spirit **(Ac. 2:1-11; 10:44-46; 19:1-6; Rom. 12:26,27; et al.)**; rather, they pertain to the congregational manifestation of the Spirit of "tongues" along with its required accompanying interpretation of tongues. Ground rules for the orderly operation of the manifestations are necessary only for their operation in the congregational forum, since it would be difficult for one to be "out of order" in the operation of the manifestations of the Spirit in his private prayer and praise activity. It would be hard to imagine how that praying, praising, or singing "in the Spirit" privately could possibly ever be "out of order".

1 Cor. 14:27 "If anyone **speaks** in a tongue...let one **interpret**"

> Every God-inspired message spoken on behalf of God in the congregational forum (prophecy, not prayer or praise) must be accompanied with interpretation into the common language of the hearers, because it is a message from God to the assembly, which cannot be understood unless it is interpreted into the common language of the hearers **(1 Cor. 14:6-17)**. If tongues are not interpreted then it is not prophecy (a message from God to the congregation), but prayer and praise. Only tongues interpreted into the common language of the hearers enabling them to understand the message and be edified by it is prophecy.

1 Cor. 14:13,28 "Therefore let one who **speaks** in a tongue pray that he may interpret...but if there is **no interpreter, let him keep silent IN THE CHURCH;** and let him **speak to himself** and to God."

> Messages in tongues should only be given when "one who interprets" is present, which may be the speaker himself.

> If no interpreter is present, then the person who has received a message from God should either pray for the interpretation if he is accustomed to interpreting messages in tongues,

or he should keep silent in the church assembly and "speak (that message) to himself" and use his tongue to praise God, rather than to give the message to the entire congregation.

1 Cor. 14:2 "For one who speaks in a **tongue** does not speak to men, but to God...."

Taken out of its full context **(verses 1-5)**, it would appear that this verse is saying that a person who speaks in tongues is speaking to God and not to men, that is, he is not speaking a message from God to the assembly. However, when coupled with the entire context, as well as when it is connected with the information in the rest of the Chapter, it becomes clear that what is being said is that an utterance in tongues without the required interpretation in the congregational forum is directed to God as prayer and praise.

1 Cor. 14:2 "...**for no one understands,** but **in his spirit** he speaks mysteries...."

The rest of this verse makes it clear that the reason that a person speaking in a tongue without interpretation is speaking to God is because "no one **understands**", and utterances in tongues spoken in the assembly as the first half of a prophetic message is intended to be understood by the congregation, which is why interpretation of tongues is then necessary and required.

Notice also the phrase "in his **spirit**". This is where a message from God communicated in tongues is initially received — within the human spirit. It is God communicating through the Holy Spirit to the human spirit of the person receiving the message. It is incumbent upon that person to then determine if this is a message that God wants communicated to the entire congregation. If there is not an interpreter present to interpret the message in tongues to the congregation (see below), then the person receiving the message in tongues "in his spirit" should "keep silent in the church (congregation)" and should "speak to himself and to God" **(1 Cor. 14:28)**. If it would be consistent with the flow of the Spirit in that service and the message would be "in order," then the person should give the message in tongues, in order for it to be interpreted to the congregation. When tongues are interpreted, the message is **no longer "a mystery"** — that is the purpose of interpretation.

So, one is speaking **to God** in a tongue, that is praying or praising, when there is no interpretation of the message into the common tongue of the congregation so that they all may understand and thus be edified. Tongues in the congregational usage is one half of prophecy, for tongues with interpretation **IS** prophecy.

All of this becomes even clearer when the first part of the full context is connected with the last part of the full context, in which case the following is the result:

> "For one who speaks in a **tongue (without interpretation)** does not speak to men, but to God; for no one understands, but in his spirit he speaks mysteries... **UNLESS HE INTERPRETS,** so that **THE CHURCH** may receive **EDIFYING.**" **(1 Cor. 14:2-5)**

A person speaking in a tongue is speaking to God in prayer and praise unless his message is interpreted, in which case he is then speaking a message from God to men for the purposes of edification of the congregation present (prophecy):

A Biblical Perspective of the Prophetic Gifts and Office

1 Cor. 14:2-4 "For one who speaks in a tongue does not speak to men, but to God; for no one understands, but in his spirit he speaks mysteries. **But one who prophesies SPEAKS TO MEN...one who prophesies edifies THE CHURCH...."**

THE FUNCTION AND FRUIT OF TONGUES:

1 Cor. 14:22 "So then tongues are for a **sign...to unbelievers**"

It is a supernatural "sign" especially to **unbelievers** (which, however, in no way infers that it is not to be manifested where only believers are present) with the same function and fruit as prophecy (see explanation given under the heading: **"THE FUNCTION AND FRUIT OF PROPHECY."**)

PRIMARY FOCUS OF THE FOURTEENTH CHAPTER OF FIRST CORINTHIANS IS THE *CONGREGATIONAL* OPERATION OF THE MANIFESTATIONS OF THE SPIRIT

Since in all practicality it is virtually impossible for an individual believer to operate these manifestations of the Spirit in any manner other than "decently and in order" in personal and private prayer and praise, the primary focus of the instruction given in **First Corinthians 14** must be concerning their operation in the congregational forum. The purpose and objective of this entire chapter is, indeed, the final and summational verse of the chapter essentially proving the delineation of the rules effecting the proper and decent operation of these "manifestations of the Spirit".

THE MANIFESTATION GIFT OF INTERPRETATION OF TONGUES

The Interpretation of Tongues (manifested in the congregational forum) simply **defined**: a supernatural God-inspired interpretation of a message given in tongues into the common language of the hearers.

1 Cor. 14:27 "If anyone **speaks** in a tongue...let one **interpret**"

Tongues given as one-half of prophecy in the assembly must **always** be interpreted.

Tongues in prayer and praise do not require an interpretation.

1 Cor. 14:2-5 "For one who speaks in a tongue does not speak to men, but to God; for no one understands, but in his spirit he speaks mysteries. But one who prophesies speaks to men...one who prophesies edifies the church...**and greater is one who PROPHESIES than one who SPEAKS IN TONGUES, *UNLESS HE INTERPRETS*...."**

Tongues **with** interpretation of tongues is equivalent to prophecy, and in fact, **IS** prophecy.

SECTION VII:

ABOUT PERSONAL PROPHECY

LESSON 22
ALL ABOUT PERSONAL PROPHECY

Though the subject of personal prophecy is by far the matter of greatest interest in regard to the prophetic realm to the vast majority of Spirit-Baptized believers, it is not the main focus of this prophetic course. However, personal prophecy is part and parcel of the present Prophetic Movement, and therefore requires some attention in a course such as this. In this Lesson is presented an **overview** of the matter of personal prophecy. Herein, the term "personal prophesy" is simply a term used to refer to prophecy given to and pertaining to an individual person.

WE *KNOW* IN PART AND *PROPHESY* IN PART.

Prophecy is comprised of partial information, fragmentary portions of Divine information. God only reveals fragmentary portions of knowledge to the prophet. Because of our finite knowledge, it is very difficult for carnal human beings to accurately interpret the infinite knowledge of God revealed or expressed in prophetic utterances. The greatest problems in the area of the prophetic lie in the matter of interpretation of what God has said. A combination of much wisdom, common sense, Bible knowledge, experience, and understanding of prophetic terminology is needed to accurately interpret prophecy. Often, some portions of prophecy cannot be properly interpreted until it begins to come to pass or God is ready to reveal it. Certainly, "interpretability" of a prophecy, either by the prophet or the recipient, especially at the time it is given, is **not** the indicator of its validity, and no prophet is **required** to interpret any prophecy the Lord has expressed through Him.

PROPHECY NEED NOT BE EXPLICIT (DETAILED) TO BE VALID OR ACCURATE

This is true whether those things being addressed pertain to the past, present, or future. The language of prophecy is often cryptic and "coded." Jesus often conveys His testimony (prophecy; **Rev. 19:10**) today in the same manner as He did in the days of His earthly ministry as recorded in the Gospels—in parables, dark sayings, riddles, cryptic conundrums. To the uninformed bystander, some personal prophecies may **seem** to be generalized and non-specific, though it rarely seems that way to the person being addressed. As a protection to prevent embarrassment and unnecessary and improper exposure, in prophecy the Lord usually only says enough about certain matters to allow the recipient to personally identify that matter He is addressing; others hearing the prophecy usually have absolutely no idea what He is talking about (unless the person to whom the prophecy is directed tells them). God rarely gives us every explicit detail regarding a future occurrence, for that would eliminate the necessity of faith. Additionally, He often will tell us **"what"**, without giving the slightest clue as to **"how,"** because it is often in the discovery of the "how" that faith is of necessity exercised and often further developed. True prophecy will never stunt our growth but will always reveal something that is hindering our spiritual development or will present a challenge to us to grow.

A Biblical Perspective of the Prophetic Gifts and Office

SECTION VII: ABOUT PERSONAL PROPHECY

PERSONAL PROPHECY IS *ALWAYS* CONDITIONAL—FULFILLMENT IS DETERMINED BY THE RECIPIENT, NOT THE PROPHET, OR EVEN GOD.

Our response to the prophecy, usually, is what will determine whether or not it is fulfilled. In this regard, it is vital that the distinction between **PERSONAL** prophecy and **GENERAL** prophecy be understood. *General* prophecy will always come to pass regardless of circumstances or human actions. *Personal* prophecy, on the other hand, is *always* conditional, and fulfillment is dependent upon the response and obedience of the person(s) to whom the prophecy is directed.

JUDGE THE *PROPHECY*, NOT THE *PROPHET*, TO DETERMINE THE VALIDITY OF THE PROPHECY.

Many people confuse the matter of the prophet with the matter of the content of the prophecy, because they have been taught so much fear regarding the prophetic area and "watching out for false prophets." The content of prophecy should be judged primarily on the basis of the Word of God and whether it exalts Jesus. So many people are so intent on judging the prophet that they never hear a word of the prophecy. Errors that are made in prophecy, especially by inexperienced "prophesiers" most frequently occur in the area of articulation of the word which they have received from God. Mistakes in articulation do sometimes occur in personal prophecy. There's only one Prophet who never missed it in prophesying—**JESUS**—and they crucified Him.

Any human being can make a mistake. Let him who has never erred cast the first stone. No prophet (other than Jesus) was ever born with perfect proficiency in his giftings. Neither are those in the other four ministry offices perfect in their gifting; no evangelist, for example, gets everyone saved, healed, and delivered. Every believer must mature spiritually and develop in his calling and in the operation of the giftings the Lord operates through him. Those called to the prophetic office, like anyone else, must be given the grace to develop in their ministry, despite their mistakes. As in every other case with developing saints, there are immature and underdeveloped prophets, who will gain more experience, proficiency, accuracy, and wisdom as they grow and develop in the Lord. However, we are, of course, aiming for excellence in the prophetic ministry.

BEWARE OF CALLING SOMEONE A "FALSE PROPHET!"

If a prophet misses it, that does not make him a "false prophet." What makes a false prophet false is not the level of proficiency or even accuracy in his prophesying, but rather the **motives and intents** of his heart and ministry (Mat. 7:15). Jesus said false prophets are false because **INWARDLY** the are ravenous (selfishly aggrandizing) wolves. The ministry of true prophets always exalts Jesus, not self. False prophets are false because it is their **HEART** that is not right, not their giftings or ministry.

The overall result of any minister's (or saint's) endeavors to allow Jesus to minister to people through them whose heart is right before God will be **"good fruit."** Those whose heart is not right and whose motives are not pure cannot produce genuinely good fruit. Beware of judging any of God's servants:

> "Who are you to **judge** the servant of another? To his own Master (Jesus) he stands or falls; and stand he will, for the Lord is able to make him stand." **(Rom. 14:4)**

A Biblical Perspective of the Prophetic Gifts and Office

"Do not **judge** lest you be judged. **For in the way you judge, you will be judged**; and by your standard of measure, it will be measured to you." **(Mat. 7:1,2)**

Unless you want to be judged by God to be false every time you miss it or make a mistake or error in judgment, you better not use that measure to judge the validity of another person's life and ministry. There **are** false prophets, but we must be sure that we use Scriptural methods to determine those who are indeed false.

THERE ARE MAJOR DIFFERENCES BETWEEN THE OFFICE OF THE PROPHET AND THE SIMPLE GIFT OF PROPHECY.

Prophecy through **"one who prophesies"** must be limited to edification, exhortation, and comfort **(1 Cor. 14:3)**. Personal prophecy through a **prophet**, however, is not so limited, but may contain **direction, guidance, foretelling of future events, divine counsel, reproof, warning, admonition,** and in certain cases even **rebuke (2 Tim. 4:2)**. The six-faceted ministry of the prophet as a watchman in the Church who is accountable to God is to: 1) **pluck up,** 2) **break down,** 3) **destroy,** 4) **overthrow,** 5) **build,** 6) **plant (Jer. 1:10)**. Prophets are **"seers" (First Samuel 9:9)**, and as such deal in **divine insight and revelation.** God has testified that He reveals His **"secret counsel"** to His servants the prophets **(Amos 3:7)**. Thus, prophecy expressed through a prophet **MAY** be confirmation, but does not have to be limited to confirmation, it **MAY** also give new revelation and insight.

NO ONE SHOULD EVER DO ANYTHING OR MAKE ANY MAJOR CHANGES IN HIS LIFE MERELY BASED ON ANY PROPHECY.

"Let every word be confirmed by the mouth of two or three witnesses" — prophets are often used by the Lord as a confirming witness of divine counsel. Major decisions should not be made without confirmation from the Lord. Prophets can often provide that confirmation in personal prophecy. However, no one should ever make any major changes in his life based solely on a personal prophecy.

TIMING IS CRITICAL!

The Prophet may not know what part of your life he is speaking about — **past, present, or future.** He may speak in present tense of a situation you went through in the past. Or, he may speak of something in the present tense that will take place in the future. The tense is not as important as the substance of the prophecy. It is important to remember that when prophetic decrees come forth, they are at that moment decreed in the spiritual realm, but they often require indeterminate further passage of time to be manifested in the natural.

Prophetic terminology regarding time is different than every day usage. For example: in **First Samuel 13:1-14**, regarding Saul losing his kingdom, **"now"** meant 38 years later; in **First Samuel 15:28**, regarding the transfer of kingship to David, **"this day"** meant 24 years later; the last recorded words of Jesus in the Bible were: **"I come QUICKLY,"** thus the term "quickly" apparently can mean **2,000 years or more**.

PERSONAL PROPHECY IS FULFILLED BY APPROPRIATE RESPONSES

Fulfillment of *personal* prophecy is dependent upon the recipient's response to the prophecy. Some appropriate responses to personal prophecy are:

1. **Record and meditate** upon your prophecy in order to use it to fight the good fight of faith — **1 Tim. 1:18**.

2. **Obey** both the Rhema and the Logos Word of God.

3. **Don't panic! Rest in the Lord!** Don't try to immediately fulfill any prophecy through self-effort, but allow God to grow you into its fulfillment. Do nothing different unless divinely directed and until you have a confirmed "knowing" within your own heart.

4. **Be patient, persevere, and endure hardship** — **Jas. 1:2-17; 5:7-11; 2 Tim. 4:5**.

5. **Believe** tested and proven prophecies given by Prophets and succeed — **2 Chron. 20:20**.

6. **War** a good warfare through profession of portions of the prophetic word made more sure—the Logos (Scripture) that confirm and comport with the prophecies you've been given — **1 Tim. 1:18; 2 Pet. 1:16-21**.

7. **Store away** those things you don't understand until a later time when God makes it clear to you. Some prophetic words given by God can remain a mystery until "the fulness of time," that is to say, until it is time for them to come to pass. There are many prophecies in Scripture which did not come to pass until many years after they were first spoken. Oftentimes, prophecy is a foretelling of future events.

8. **Eat the hay and spit out the sticks.** Under the New Testament dispensation, God uses imperfect vessels to speak forth prophecy on His behalf, just as He uses imperfect vessels to operate other manifestations of the Spirit. The New Covenant is one of mercy, grace, and love rather than law and retribution as was the Old Covenant. Those who have the fortitude to be used by God prophetically, must be given the grace to grow and mature in their spiritual giftings. At times, those who are immature in the prophetic giftings, spiritually, or in their communication skills, can and do speak things that are not 100% accurate, Scriptural, discreet, or well-spoken. Yet, we must not allow such occurrences or prospects to stifle or stop the operation of the prophetic gifts, for they edify the church **(1 Cor. 14:3,4)**, and thus are greatly needed.

    "Do not **quench** (suppress or subdue) the (Holy) Spirit. Do not **spurn** the gifts and utterances of the prophets—do not **depreciate** prophetic revelations nor **despise** inspired instruction or exhortation or warning. But test and prove all things [until you recognize] what is good; [to that] hold fast" **(1 Thes. 5:19-21, A.B.)**.